WAR AND PEACE
IN THE MIDDLE EAST

WAR AND PEACE
IN THE MIDDLE EAST

✳ ✳ ✳ ✳

*The Experiences and Views
of a U.N. Observer*

BY

GENERAL ODD BULL

LEO COOPER
LONDON

First Published by Gyldendal Norsk Forlag, Oslo, 1973
First Published in this edition 1976 by
LEO COOPER LTD.
196 Shaftesbury Avenue, London WC2H 8JL

Copyright © 1973 and 1976 Odd Bull

ISBN 0 85052 226 9

Printed in Great Britain by
Western Printing Services Ltd
Bristol

****

Dedicated to
Eric Sixstenson Sparre
Thomas Wickham
Bo Roland Plane
Jens Emil Alfred Bögvad

WHO GAVE THEIR LIVES
IN THE SERVICE OF PEACE

****

CONTENTS

ILLUSTRATIONS

* * * *

MAPS

❀ ❀ ❀ ❀

1. Jerusalem
2. Israel—Syria—Jordan
3. Israel—Lebanon—Syria
4. Israel—Egypt

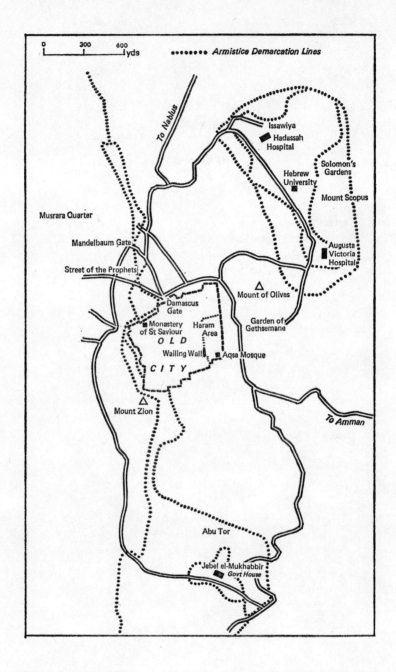

0   300   600
|—|—|—|yds   •••••• *Armistice Demarcation Lines*

To Nablus

Issawiya
Hadassah
Hospital

Solomon's
Gardens

Hebrew
University

Mount Scopus

Musrara Quarter

Augusta
Victoria
Hospital

Mandelbaum Gate

Street of the Prophets

△
Mount of Olives

Damascus
Gate

Monastery
of St Saviour

Haram
Area

Garden of
Gethsemane

O L D

Wailing Wall

Aqsa Mosque

C I T Y

△
Mount Zion

To Amman

Abu Tor

Jebel el-Mukhabbir
Govt House

SYRIA

Tel el-Qadi
Baniyas
R. Dan
Golan Heights
R. Baniyas
Hasbani
Quneitra
OP Bravo
Naqura
OP Charlie
Lake Huleh
Ghanname
Khouri Farm
Banat Yacub Bridge
Mahanayim
Rafid
Almagor
OP Delta
Capernaum
Lake Tiberias
OP Foxtrot
Tiberias
Ein Gev
Yarmuk

ISRAEL
Baggara

Afula
Irbid

Megiddo
Muqeibila
Jenin

Jordan

Tulkarm
JORDAN

Ramat Hakoresh
Nablus
Qalqiliya

Damia Bridge
Zerka

El-Karameh
Amman

Ramallah
Shuna

Beit Nuba
Jericho
Allenby Bridge
Latrun
Yalu
Ein Karem
Jerusalem

0   5   10   20 miles
   10   30 km

Dead
Sea

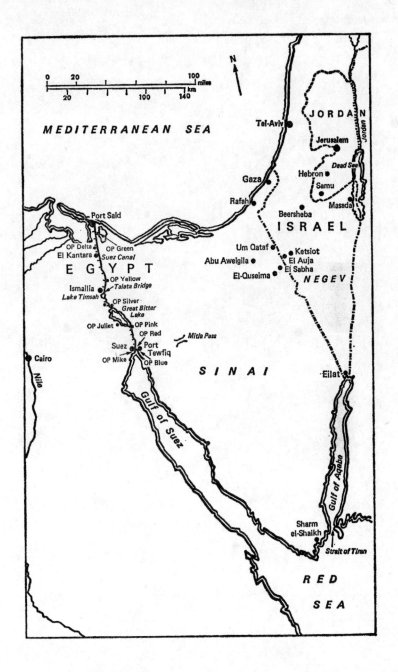

FOREWORD

✳ ✳ ✳ ✳

Many people have from time to time urged me to write my memoirs, but I only decided to do so when I came back to Norway at Christmas, 1967, and found that public opinion there regarded the Palestine problem almost entirely from the Israeli point of view. As this was a problem with which I had been living for many years, and one which, as I had become very much aware, had at least two sides to it, I felt in conscience bound to make my own experience the basis for as calm and objective a presentation of the whole Middle East situation as I could. For those from outside who, like myself, have become involved in this situation the aim must always be to try to reduce the burden of suffering and injustice for all people in that area, Arabs and Israelis alike.

I spent more than seven years in the Middle East, not counting an apprenticeship of six months in Lebanon in 1958. These seven years were sharply divided by the June War of 1967. From June, 1963, till June, 1967, my main task as United Nations Truce Supervisor was to attempt to deal with the conflicts which arose along the armistice lines between Israel and Jordan and Israel and Syria. The border between Israel and Lebanon was quiet and so, thanks to the presence there after the Suez campaign of 1956 of the United Nations Emergency Force, was the border between Israel and Egypt. After the 1967 war everything changed. The immediate task of the UN then was to re-establish a ceasefire line between Israel and Syria and to get the observer team there working again, and subsequently to arrange for a new observer network in the Suez Canal area, which had now become the ceasefire line between the Israeli and Egyptian forces. It was this second part of our task which was to prove much the more intractable.

I have also thought it proper to include in this book a chapter on the Lebanon crisis of 1958, and I hope that English-speaking readers may find something to interest them in a brief chapter recounting my early service career and my experiences in the war. In the Norwegian version I included a fairly long chapter called 'Historical Background' as most Norwegians have little understanding about how the problems of the Middle East, particularly that of Palestine, arose. But I have omitted this for English-speaking readers who are more familiar with this chapter of history.

Finally I am greatly indebted to E. C. Hodgkin for his very valuable assistance in preparing this book.

CHAPTER 1

LEBANESE OVERTURE

On Thursday, 12 June, 1958, I was in my house just about to go for a walk when the telephone rang. It was General B. F. Motzfeldt, Chief of Air Staff, on the line. He began to talk about the deteriorating situation in Lebanon. I knew that the Secretary-General of the United Nations, Dag Hammarskjöld, had asked Norway for the loan of the services in Lebanon of General Hansteen, Commandant of the National Defence College, and I thought that probably General Motzfeldt was going to ask me to take over General Hansteen's job temporarily while he was away. But I was mistaken. Apparently General Hansteen was unable, for private reasons, to accept, and now Motzfeldt was asking if I would consider going to Lebanon as member of a UN observer group. He wanted my answer in half an hour.

The proposal both surprised and pleased me. The work was a challenge which appealed to me as a professional soldier, and the fact that the offer came from Hammarskjöld increased its attractiveness. I discussed the idea with my wife, who encouraged me to accept, and within half an hour I had rung Motzfeldt back to tell him of my acceptance.

Now things began to move with great speed. When the Security Council does agree on a resolution it usually wants to see it put into operation as quickly as possible. The next day, Friday, the 13th, I had a talk with the Secretary of State at the Foreign Office, Hans Engen, who had for many years been head of Norway's delegation to the UN and was a close personal friend of Hammarskjöld. He explained to me the situation in Lebanon and the background to the Security Council debate. I spent the rest of the day reading everything I could lay my hands on which had to do with Lebanon, since my knowledge of that country was minimal.

It had been agreed that I should leave on Sunday, but that evening, while I was with some friends near Oslo, I was called to the 'phone. It was Fridtjof Jacobsen of the Norwegian Foreign Office; he had just been talking to Hammarskjöld who said he would be very disappointed if I was not on my way by the next morning. I told Jacobsen that if he could produce the passport and the ticket I was ready. So it was that on Saturday morning I found myself on a SAS plane bound for my first mission in the service of the UN.

The UN operation in Lebanon was in one way unique since, for the first time, the UN had become involved in a country where a civil war was being fought. Normally, of course, the UN is forbidden by its charter to interfere in the internal affairs of any member country, but the circumstances in Lebanon were so exceptional that they require some explanation.

Lebanon is a small country, about the size of Wales, with a narrow coastal plain backed by two mountain ranges, Lebanon and Anti-Lebanon, themselves separated by the fertile Bekaa valley. To the north and east lies Syria and to the south Israel. The total population of the country in 1958 was about 1,500,000, of whom about 165,000 were refugees from Palestine. About half the population is Moslem and the other half Christian of various sects, the majority being Maronites, a Uniate (Catholic) Church with its own oriental rite. An important minority are the Druzes, mountain folk with a formidable reputation as warriors, who split off from Islam to follow their own secret religion in the twelfth century. In order to preserve the balance between the various communities, and so the unity of the state, an understanding was reached before Lebanon achieved its independence in 1945 that the communities should be equally represented in Government and public offices. By convention the President of the country is always a Maronite, the Prime Minister always a Sunni Moslem, the President of the Chamber a Shii Moslem, and so on.

But now Lebanon was in a condition approaching civil war. What had gone wrong? The President was Camille Chamoun,

2

who had taken office in 1952. An extremely able and forceful man, he made no secret of his sympathies with the West. During the Suez crisis of 1956 he gave Nasser no support, and when the fighting began he failed to follow the lead of other Arab Governments who broke off relations with Britain and France. When Eisenhower launched his 'Eisenhower Doctrine' in 1957, which promised economic and military aid for any Arab country prepared to make a stand against 'international communism', Lebanon was almost the only country to welcome it. Throughout 1957 opposition to Chamoun from Arab Nationalist admirers of Nasser inside Lebanon, mostly Moslems, mounted. There were complaints that parliamentary elections had been rigged in favour of Chamoun's supporters. Such complaints had been heard before, but what caused the pot to boil over was a growing suspicion that Chamoun intended to set aside, or secure an amendment to, the provisions in the constitution which forbade a President to stand for a second term of office. Elections for a new Parliament were due on 24 July, but in May a journalist belonging to an opposition (Moslem) paper was murdered and fighting broke out.

The unique character of Lebanon is shown by what happened next. Anywhere else the President, if he had the army on his side, would have sent it in to crush the rebels; or, if the army was against him, he would have been overthrown. But in Lebanon the army, like other institutions, was balanced between the religious communities and was not prepared to take sides. The army commander, General Fuad Chehab,* an able and wise man who had been prominent in the affairs of Lebanon since independence, was perfectly clear on this point. He was\a Christian, and he knew that if the army got drawn into a civil war it would disintegrate. The most he could do was to give a clear warning that if the rebels went beyond certain clearly defined points they would be stopped. This warning was put into effect when a group of rebels came too near Beirut on the heights to the south of the city; General Chehab then showed his teeth, whereupon, as our observers were to report, the rebels withdrew.

* The Chehab family has played a leading part in Lebanese history: it has Christian, Moslem and even Druze branches.

In this situation President Chamoun had to look outside his own country for help, and the natural place for him to look was the West. For its part the opposition looked for help across the borders to Nasser's United Arab Republic—Egypt and Syria had earlier that year agreed on a complete union between their two countries under this name. So it was that the affairs of Lebanon became internationalized.

Chamoun maintained that the opposition was receiving aid, both of men and weapons, from over the Syrian border, and it was on this ground that the Lebanese Government had brought the matter before the Security Council. In spite of protests from the opposition that this was purely an internal matter the Council agreed to consider the complaint and a resolution put forward by Dr Gunnar Jarring, the Swedish delegate, was passed on 11 June by a large majority, the Soviet Union abstaining. The resolution called for the urgent dispatch of an observer group to check on the infiltration of men and material across the border with Syria and so became the mandate for the establishment of the United Nations Observer Group in Lebanon (UNOGIL). On 12 June the Secretary-General named the three members of the Group—Galo Plaza, former President of Equador; Rajeshwar Dayal, the Indian Ambassador to Yugoslavia; and Major-General Odd Bull of Norway, who was appointed 'executive member in charge of military observers'.

On Saturday, 14 June I got no further towards my goal than Ankara. Reports had come in of serious fighting in Beirut and the SAS pilot was unwilling to land there in the dark. The next morning fighting was reported to have slacked off somewhat and we resumed our journey, landing at Beirut airport shortly before 5 am on 15 June. Because of the fighting the day before nobody had received news of my impending arrival; consequently there was no one at the airport to meet me. But I managed to get hold of a station wagon and so reached the Biarritz Hotel in Ras Beirut, which was to be the group's temporary headquarters.

My first contacts were with Leif Edwardsen, Secretary at the Norwegian Embassy in Egypt, who had been placed at my disposal by the Norwegian Foreign Office, David Blicken-

4

staff, Secretary of the Group, and Lt-Colonel M. Brown of New Zealand, seconded from the United Nations Truce Supervision Organization (UNTSO). The first military observers had arrived in Beirut three days earlier in white jeeps lent by UNTSO in Jerusalem. I was brought up to date with the latest situation and later in the morning we had a meeting with General Von Horn, the Chief of Staff of UNTSO, and Andrew Cordier, a political adviser and one of Hammarskjöld's closest colleagues. These two had come from Jerusalem to see if they could be of any help. Before they arrived Von Horn had sent me a cheerful message: 'My job is impossible and insoluble. I dare say yours will be even more so.'

According to its mandate from the Security Council UNOGIL had no police function. All it could do was 'observe and report'. Nor could it concern itself with anything that had happened before it came into being. At our first meeting we discussed the number of observers we should need, communications, and whether the observers should be armed. At the end of the meeting I telegraphed to Hammarskjöld asking for a hundred observers, for light recce planes and helicopters, and recommending that the observers should not be armed. My argument was that if observers were allowed to carry arms for self-defence this would inevitably become known to both sides who would, if they fired, shoot to kill, whereas if it was known that the observers were unarmed the combatants would probably be content with warning shots. This proved to be the case.

Our meeting went on all morning, and during one of its breaks Cordier and Blickenstaff were talking together by a window when two shots rang out. Both bullets struck just below the sill—a miss of about 15cm. Had the shots been a fraction higher one or both would have been hit in the stomach. We never found out which side it was that sent us this particular greeting.

Later in the day I paid a courtesy visit on President Chamoun to write my name in his visitors' book, but I found myself invited in for an audience. Chamoun was a most impressive figure and his manner was friendly. He gave me his version of the events and made it abundantly clear that he expected UNOGIL to act in support of himself and his

Government. I contented myself with explaining the mandate which I had received from the Security Council. The same day I received a letter from the Prime Minister, Sami es-Solh, telling me that a committee of liaison between the Government and UNOGIL had been set up under the Minister of Health, Dr Albert Mokheiber.

The next few days were spent in getting down to work, and it was with a considerable surprise that on 18 June we learned that Hammarskjöld was going to visit us in person. It was to be several years before I found out what lay behind this decision. Apparently Chamoun was dissatisfied with the way things were working out. Although it was quite unrealistic to expect that the UN would agree to send troops to Lebanon, since any such proposal would have been met by a Soviet veto, this is what he had been hoping for. He considered an observer corps as completely inadequate, and when he realized its limitations he turned secretly to the United States, citing the Eisenhower Doctrine. The Americans were anxious to do what they could to back up Chamoun's régime but were uncertain how to act. While they were still hesitating Hammarskjöld got wind of Chamoun's request and determined to do all he could to prevent any unilateral American intervention.

Hammarskjöld arrived in Beirut on 19 June, which enabled him to attend the first full meeting of the observer group, at which Galo Plaza was elected chairman. He had meetings with President Chamoun, the Prime Minister and General Chehab. From Beirut he went on to Cairo for talks with President Nasser. As a result of Hammarskjöld's flying visit the US apparently concluded that grounds for intervention by it in Lebanon did not exist.*

The politician at the head of the forces opposed to the President was Saab Salam, a former Prime Minister, who headed a junta which had its headquarters in the Basta district of Beirut, though the opposition could also count on support from armed groups spread throughout the country. These were

* One evening around this time I was having dinner with the American Ambassador, R. McClintock. After dinner he drew me to one side, pointed to the telephone, and said, 'This gives me a direct line to the American Sixth Fleet. Do you think I should call them in?' I told him I thought this was an extremely bad idea.

mostly headed by local politicians and tribal leaders and there was little co-ordination between them, nor did they have any radio communication. In fact the opposition had little organization above platoon level, so that there was never any prospect of their putting up much show against the army, should it have come to that. The best trained and best organized opposition forces were those under the control of the Druze leader, Kamal Jumblatt, in the Chouf region. Jumblatt had been at the Sorbonne, was a great admirer of Indian philosophy and of Gandhi, a practitioner of yoga and a friend of my Indian colleague, Dayal. His military adviser and, so we assumed, the commander of the Druze armed forces, was Chucat Chucair, who had at one time been Syrian Chief of Staff, though a Lebanese citizen.

The opposition was divided in its attitude towards Nasser. The majority assured us that they wished Lebanon to continue free and independent and just wanted to get rid of Chamoun. But when the Prime Minister, Sami es-Solh, issued a statement that Chamoun would not seek any amendment to the constitution the opposition insisted that he should resign straight away. This he was not willing to do. So matters stood at the beginning of July, and probably a way out could have been found, since UNOGIL had already had a marked calming effect, had it not been for the coup in Baghdad on 14 July in which the King and most of his family and the Prime Minister, Nuri es-Said, were murdered.

* * *

How did the UN observer group set about its task? As I have already pointed out, its function was not in any sense to act as a policeman; it was simply there to observe and report. To this end it was initially equipped with a hundred officers and with some reconnaissance planes and helicopters. Within the limits of our mandate we had a very free hand, though in view of the complexity of the situation with which we had to deal few rated our chances of success high. When the Security Council passed its resolution on 11 June Hammarskjöld is reported to have said he thought we had perhaps a ten per cent chance of pulling it off. But after his visit to Beirut later in the month he

7

told us he thought the odds in our favour had risen to about 50–50.

When I met Hammarskjöld on 19 June I put forward a request for an intelligence officer. This was approved, and a few days later a Norwegian, Major Overdale, arrived. After a month he was completely worn out by his exertions and was replaced on 2 August by Lt-Colonel L. Heyerdahl, whose initial task was to check the first report which we had recently sent to the Security Council. After careful investigation he came to the conclusion that the picture presented in the report was a fair one. That someone with such a reputation for impartiality as Colonel Heyerdahl should come to this conclusion was encouraging for all members of the group—encouragement which they were to need, after the strong criticism which had been fired at the group when its first report was made public.

When it was a question of reports on incidents sent in by our own observers we could always summon them for further questioning, to make sure that we got as accurate a picture as possible, and this we conscientiously did. But it was a different matter when the incidents were first reported by Government sources. These usually gave an alarming account of intervention from abroad, and in several cases we pressed for more detail, but without ever getting an answer. To give an example of the sort of material with which we had to deal I might mention one particular case which was to cause us a good deal of trouble. A Government report spoke of 'two prominent persons' who had been apprehended after infiltrating into Lebanon (Charles Malik, Lebanon's representative on the Security Council, referred to them as 'officers'), and the affair sounded so potentially serious that I decided to take a personal part in their interrogation. It quickly became clear that these two 'important persons' were two Moslems aged 21 and 17, both of whom were illiterate, and had come to Lebanon to seek seasonal employment, as the older one had in fact done for the past five years. When the fighting started they had, for reasons of personal safety, moved into the predominantly Moslem Basta district where they had been recruited to take part in an action on 14 June. This was not the only occasion

8

when our interpretation of what was meant by 'important persons' differed from that of the Government.

From the outset we formed the strong impression that the Lebanese Government wanted to make use of us for its own ends, hoping that we should expose a situation which would justify its demand for military intervention. When we failed to come up to the Government's expectations relations between it and us became cool, and eventually could only be described as icy. In papers friendly to the Government we were the target for daily abuse, and this abuse was uncritically picked up and reproduced in a large part of the foreign press. I could hardly open a newspaper which did not carry stories about the stupidity and dishonesty of the UN group and about the squabbles which were supposed to be going on inside it. It is therefore worth recording that at no time was there any disagreement inside the group on any important subject. On the contrary, from the outset co-operation within the group was outstanding and its members became excellent friends. I had, and have, the greatest respect for my two former colleagues.

The basic cause of disagreement between us and the Lebanese Government was that it claimed there was continuous infiltration from Syria, whereas our observers showed that in fact there was very little. It could be argued that this was just a case of one assertion against another, so perhaps some more detail should be given of how we operated on our side. The first observers, seconded from UNTSO, arrived in Lebanon on 12 June; the first of the newly recruited observers arrived five days later. Within a few days of the Security Council's resolution UN stations had been set up in Beirut, Tripoli, Merjayoun and Chtoura, the latter under Lt-Colonel Stig Mauritz Möllersward.* Later additional stations were established in Saida and Baalbek.

---

* In his native Sweden Colonel Möllersward had long been a legend, even though he had never risen above the rank of Rittmastere (Captain). A regular cavalry officer, always immaculately dressed, he had fought with great gallantry with the Swedish contingent in both Finnish wars. At various times subsequently he served in a number of UN commands, and was promoted to Lt-Colonel. After retiring from the army he became Swedish Consul-General in Jerusalem. He had earlier become a Roman Catholic, but won the respect of all Christian communities in the Holy City and of the Moslems. He died in 1967.

No sooner had we got down to work in earnest than we came up against an unexpected snag; the opposition refused to allow UN observers access to the border areas, arguing that any trouble there was purely an internal Lebanese affair. After a bit the opposition changed its tactics and said it was willing to issue the observers with passes. This we refused, since we considered that our white jeeps should be themselves sufficient passes. This was accepted and we thought our problems solved. But not for the last time we were to discover that the acceptance of something in principle was not the end of the story. When it was a case of dealing with subordinate opposition leaders in the rural areas the whole negotiating process had to be gone through again. The border between Lebanon and Syria is about 325km long, and to all intents and purposes the opposition controlled the whole of it. Not a word of this had been breathed in the Security Council debates and the Lebanese Government itself was not surprisingly reluctant to explain to us how matters really stood. So we had to find out for ourselves.

The only thing we could do about this long frontier, part of which lay in difficult mountain terrain, was, as a first step, to institute a daily shuttle of reconnaissance planes. The next step was to set up subsidiary stations and observation posts in all areas where infiltration over the border was likely. But even with the opposition co-operating 'in principle' it was a long time before we could claim that our observation was effective.

The sort of difficulties we were up against can be illustrated by an extract from a report by one of the observers, Major Berge: 'One of our vehicles having been mined on a road leading to the headquarters of the opposition leader in the area, a man called Shibbly, at a place called Deir el-Ashaier on the border, south of the Beirut–Damascus road, we discussed the best way of getting in contact with him. It was suggested that we should try a route they were unlikely to expect us to use. This led through very inaccessible country. Paul Wickberg and I were detailed for the job.

'We set off early in the morning in blistering heat and were in the saddle continuously for four hours. Mule riding is quite pleasant, and the sight of Wickberg on ahead whistling a marching song with his mule's bridle in one hand and a huge white flag in the other was very stimulating. The route proved to have been well chosen. We were in fact only 1 km from Shibbly's hideout when we were detected and taken prisoner by some armed shepherds who were swaggering around in their characteristic baggy trousers. We were taken to Shibbly's house where we were served coffee by the host himself in very small cups held, as is the custom, between three fingers of the right hand. With the help of Shibbly's lieutenant, who acted as interpreter, our meeting went off well, and when Wickberg asked if he might take his photograph Shibbly arose from the carpet on which we were sitting, twisted his black beard into a spiral, draped himself with some more weapons and an ammunition belt, and said "mabsut" —"content".'

Shortly after this incident the UN was able to set up observation posts along the Syrian border, all in Shibbly's area.

Then came the Baghdad coup. As we learned later it appears that President Chamoun had asked Nuri es-Said for some form of military support. Nuri agreed, and ordered units, including one commanded by Brigadier Abdul Karim Qasim, to move through Baghdad towards the Syrian frontier. In the early morning of 14 July Brigadier Qasim took this chance to carry out a coup by which the Iraq monarchy was destroyed and a military régime set up.

To say that these events heightened tension in Lebanon would be an understatement. Every sort of rumour was flying around, particularly that intervention by the US was imminent. We agreed that, should this happen, we would cease all our operations, do our best to ensure the safety of the observers, and await further developments.

On the morning of the following day, 15 July, my two colleagues went to Tripoli to meet the leader of the opposition, Rashid Karami, later to become Prime Minister. I went myself to Hermel in the northern Bekaa to meet the leader of the opposition in that area, Sabri Hamade, who was also Speaker of Parliament. Both meetings were concerned with freedom of movement for our observers in the border areas. On my way back from Hermel, at about 5.30 in the evening,

I was met by one of our patrols who informed me that American troops had landed at about 2 o'clock that afternoon in the area of the airport, south of Beirut. I went on to Chtoura, one of our main stations, to ensure that my earlier orders to suspend all operations were being followed.

Soon after my return to Beirut I had a meeting with my two colleagues. We all regarded the American landings with the utmost concern. We had become convinced that the opposition leaders were anxious for peace and that the internal situation could be resolved through the medium of the presidential election due on 24 July. It seemed clear that this would produce a new President whom the opposition could accept. Both our meetings, with Rashid Karami and Sabri Hamade, had been successful, giving us free access to the border areas. But now nobody could say what was going to happen. There was moreover some immediate danger for our observers since rumours were spreading that they had been acting as a sort of advance guard for the Americans.

During the night of 16 July we received a telegram from Hammarskjöld instructing us as to what our attitude to the Americans should be. On the basis of this telegram we issued a communiqué the next day to the effect that UNOGIL operated under mandate from the Security Council and felt itself in no way obliged to co-operate with any persons except those with whom it was already in contact. At a meeting of the group that morning we agreed to stay at our posts for as long as the UN had any use for us. One of us suggested we should all send in our resignations, but later withdrew this suggestion.

Later in the morning we had, at his request, a meeting with the American Ambassador, R. McClintock. He read us a long telegram from the American Secretary of State, John Foster Dulles, in which he emphasized the importance of UNOGIL's continuing its operations in Lebanon but urged that it should act in co-operation with the American forces. We referred the Ambassador to our communiqué, maintaining that it was impossible for us to co-operate with the Americans and that the UN would be unable to continue to operate in Lebanon if the Americans occupied the country.

Eventually an acceptable compromise was reached: the

American troops would confine themselves to the Beirut area, while UNOGIL would continue its operations in the rest of the country, particularly in the border areas. These operations began again on 17 July. This arrangement worked out quite well in practice. Presumably if the UN had in fact pulled out of Lebanon the Americans would have had to occupy the whole country, which would have raised a host of new and grave problems. On the whole the Americans kept their side of the bargain, except for an occasional reconnaissance flight along the border, which undoubtedly made things harder for our observers there. But although the American landings had been a severe setback for the UN presence we were gradually able to re-establish confidence. Much credit must go to the Commander of the American forces, Admiral Holloway, who set up his headquarters in a warship in Beirut harbour. He was the best type of naval officer and quickly had the measure of the problem confronting him.

When the whole operation was over General Chehab told me that the first forty-eight hours after the American landing had been the most difficult time in his life. Reaction by the opposition had been predictably strong, but with great skill the general had upheld morale inside the Army, and thereby for a time kept the country as a whole together. The opposition leader, Saab Salam, was induced to hold his hand. What happened was this. The first American troops were supposed to enter Beirut at 1000 hours on 16 July, but in fact arrived several hours later. The delay was due to the fact that when the advance troops reached a point a little way inside the city they were met by a jeep filled with Lebanese officers who curtly informed them that if they crossed over a designated line the Lebanese forces would open fire. The Americans halted, and when they did later enter the city it was after negotiations had been conducted between the two sides and formal permission for entry granted. This symbolic act of opposition by Lebanese forces had a considerable effect on morale in the Army and in the country as a whole.

All the same the situation remained extremely tense. On 17 July Robert Murphy, one of Dulles's leading trouble-shooters, arrived in Beirut for a personal study of the situation. He conferred with representatives of both the Government and the opposition, his aim being, to put it bluntly, to decide how far the US should go in its support for President Chamoun. He came to the conclusion that the Presidential election should go ahead as planned.

For a short time after the landing it looked as though Chamoun would try to take advantage of the new situation. He succeeded as a start in getting the election put off from 24 July to 31 July. Then on 29 July there was an attempt on the life of the Prime Minister, Sami es-Solh, and Chamoun tried to use this as an excuse to put off the elections still further, but in fact they took place on the 31st as planned and the new President was General Chehab.

It soon became clear that this change did not automatically solve all problems, as the optimists had hoped. So far the observer group had sent the Secretary-General two reports on its work, dated 3 and 30 July. These had been subjected to a good deal of criticism, both by the Lebanese Government and by Western politicians, and newspapers. One particular focus of criticism was a passage in the report of 3 July, which was perhaps unhappily phrased. It ran: 'Neither was it possible to ascertain whether any of the armed men who had been observed had infiltrated into Lebanon. There seemed very little doubt that the large majority were Lebanese.' The Lebanese Government made a great deal of play with this, asking how observers were able to tell the difference between a Lebanese and a Syrian unless they asked to see their identification papers. But in the end the report was proved to have been correct.

When we became operational again, after the landings, we began some night operations. I had consulted General Chehab about this and he had advised against it, but all the same we made a cautious start and within a few weeks observation was operating on a 24-hour basis. To give some idea of the obstacles that had to be overcome I will let one of the observers speak for himself. Here is Major Berge again:

'The opposition was most numerous and best organized in north-east Lebanon* where all positions held by Government

---

* This is not so: the opposition led by Kamal Jumblatt was the best organized.

forces had been destroyed or evacuated. We worked our way steadily northwards in this area and eventually reached Hermel, the most northerly town and near the Syrian border. After a number of attempts, and a good deal of enthusiastic shooting by the opposition, we finally got into the town and set ourselves up in a house which in more peaceful conditions had served as a school. People soon started pouring in with the most extraordinary collection of allegations and rumours. One of these was to the effect that if we failed to leave the area before dark we should be "disposed of". After a short council of war our leader, the Swedish Major Wickberg, decided that we should stay and see what happened.

'It was not an auspicious start. While we were having dinner a hail of stones the size of apples fell on the table and an armed man smashed one of our chairs because we gave him no cigarettes. It was all extremely unpleasant, and when darkness fell none of us felt like going to bed. At 1 am there was a loud noise, the door burst open, and in walked three armed men, with bayonets fixed on their rifles. They stood us up against the wall and began prodding us with their bayonets. For several minutes we stood, waiting to be shot, but eventually our assailants decided to simply strip us of all our possessions. After another council of war we decided that we had had enough, and at dawn we left. Next day all five officers in our party decided unanimously that we must make another attempt, so we went into Hermel again.'

If the observers had been armed, even only for self-defence, it is very unlikely that any of this group would have got out of Hermel alive. When they all entered Hermel for the second time they took up their headquarters again in the same school house, but this time they took with them a nephew of Saab Salam who bore a message for the local opposition leader. From that day we had a team in Hermel. It was by methods such as these that we talked our way forward in the border areas and managed to set up an effective observer system.

At the end of July our doctor reported that the observers were overworked and exhausted and that some of them would have to be sent home. The report was perhaps unduly pessimistic, but it had certainly been hard going from the first day.

15

In addition to the unique political circumstances in which we found ourselves we had to contend with the intense heat, the poor food, the isolation, and the continuous barrage of criticism to which we were subjected. President Chamoun told the Press that the observers were unfitted for their task, and lay on the beaches all day, or went to the mountains on holiday. There was not, of course, a scrap of truth in these accusations, but they were uncritically taken up by a large part of the world's Press. The observers began to get letters from home asking what they were really up to. At our insistence the liaison committee Chamoun had set up issued a *démenti*, but the damage had been done. So it was comforting to receive on 26 July a telegram from Hammarskjöld in the course of which he said: 'I have had the privilege of seeing your work at first hand, and I know that many of you, on patrol and in reconnaissance flights by day and by night, have run risks as great as any that have been met by those in the service of the UN. I can assure you that the services rendered by you in the cause of peace are greatly appreciated by the UN and by myself as Secretary-General.'

After the election was over the atmosphere became calmer, though the opposition stepped up its demands for the withdrawal of American Forces. Discussions in the Security Council got nowhere, and so a special session of the General Assembly was called for 8 August. Three resolutions were put forward, one by the Soviet Union, one by Norway, and finally, on 21 August, one by the Arab States. There was no vote on the first two, but the third was passed unanimously. This resolution gave the Secretary-General wide powers to take any steps needed to hasten a solution of the conflict and a withdrawal of American Forces. On 18 August the American Secretary of State sent the President of the Assembly a letter in which he said that American Forces would be withdrawn when this was requested by the Lebanese Government or when, as a result of further measures taken by the UN, this presence was no longer necessary. Reliance on the formula 'leave it to Dag' had never been more marked. What Hammarskjöld did was to follow up UNOGIL's suggestion to increase the strength of the observer corps to 888 officers. This was not implemented before the changeover of Presidents on 23 September, by which time the situation in the country had greatly improved, and infiltration was at an end. There was therefore no need for the extra number of observers, and in fact their total never exceeded 592, drawn from 21 different countries, and distributed between 49 stations and sub-stations. In the air, we had, by the end of the operation, twelve reconnaissance planes and six helicopters.

Our communications worked well. From our headquarters in Beirut we were in direct contact by telephone and W/T with our main stations, and these in turn were in contact with the sub-stations, observation posts, jeeps on patrol and planes in the air. Contact with the Secretary-General in New York was maintained via the UNTSO link.

By these means we obtained increasingly reliable information about the extent of infiltration taking place. How many infiltrators succeeded in crossing from Syria it is, of course, impossible to tell. But towards the end of our time, after General Chehab had taken over as President, and when we had a good deal of freedom to check all the available evidence, we came to the conclusion that probably not more than 1,100 had come in; probably two-thirds of whom were Druzes. I asked a number of leading Lebanese for their estimates, and these varied between 3,000 and 1,000. These figures should be compared with those put out by the propaganda department of Chamoun's Government. As early as 10 June it was being said that 15,000 men had been recruited in Syria for service in Lebanon and that most of them were already across the border. How many had been recruited we naturally could not tell, but I think we gained a pretty accurate idea of the number who crossed over.

Had the 1,100 (or even a smaller number) been properly trained troops they could have posed a major problem. We know that 240 men were picked up by the Government forces and deported to Syria, because their re-crossing of the border was observed by our men. We reckoned that fifteen to twenty members of the Norwegian wartime underground Linge company could have carried out the sabotage operations these men were said to have been charged with, and this made us suspect that their main function had been to strengthen the defences of the 'Basta fortress'.

*   *   *

The new President, General Chehab, took over on 23 September. An armistice was arranged and we felt that the problems which had brought us to Lebanon were on the way to solution and that the UN's task was virtually complete. The Americans appeared to share this view. They had already withdrawn some units in early September, and by 25 September their last troops had left the country. But not everything went as smoothly as we had hoped. Chehab asked Rashid Karami, who, as already mentioned, had been leader of the opposition in the Tripoli area, to form a Government, and this was resented by the half of the population which had remained loyal to Chamoun. A Christian party, the Falange, precipitated a new crisis which was, in effect, a continuation of the civil war, though with roles reversed. This time it was Beirut which suffered most, and there were daily murders, woundings and kidnappings. UN observers were often called upon to act as witnesses to what was happening.

In these circumstances the wisdom of not arming the observers became once again apparent. For example, Major Boldt, a Finn, and Captains Sollenberg and Rittby, both Swedes, were on their way to Headquarters one morning when they saw a man lying wounded in a car surrounded by an angry mob. He had been hit by three or four bullets but was still alive, and the mob wanted to finish him off by setting light to the car. One of the crowd had actually started to beat him to death. The three observers stepped in at once, and in spite of hysterical protests by the crowd managed to get him to hospital. They undoubtedly saved his life, and later they and UNOGIL were warmly thanked by the man's family. In many ways this was the most unpleasant part of our time in Lebanon, because it looked as if the situation could easily deteriorate into a straight conflict between Christians and Moslems. But at the eleventh hour the Lebanese, who seemed to be past-masters at this sort of thing, managed to find a way out. On the night of 14/15 October Karami formed a Government consisting of only four members, two Christians and two Moslems. Strictly speaking this was unconstitutional, but it worked, and Parliament later voted it the necessary authority. After this peace descended on the land almost overnight, except for the usual quota of family and tribal feuds, which had multiplied thanks to the unsettled conditions of the past months. It was a sign of the respect that the UN observers had won for themselves that they were often asked to mediate in these conflicts also.

By the end of its time UNOGIL was patrolling up to 16,000km a day in jeeps, and in addition there were foot, horse and mule patrols, as well as a 24-hour air reconnaissance. It was interesting to note the peacemaking effect these patrols had on the population, which only a few weeks earlier had been at loggerheads. Some figures are worth quoting. By November observers had been shot at 67 times, but never hit. Planes had been fired on 59 times and nine hits registered; in two of these cases the pilot was injured, though not seriously. 2,850 hours of operational flying had been clocked up. Our jeeps had averaged only one breakdown every 23,000km.

Our final report to the Security Council expressed the opinion that UNOGIL's mission had been accomplished and suggested that the observer corps could now be wound up. The Security Council confirmed this after the Lebanese Government had, on 25 November, asked for its initial complaint to be withdrawn. On 2 November Hammarskjöld told us that our own withdrawal might begin. I issued an order of the day in which I informed the observers of the Secretary-General's decision and thanked all concerned for a job well done. On 29 November a telegram came from Hammarskjöld giving unqualified praise to UNOGIL's achievement. Later I received a personal letter of thanks from him as well as messages from other quarters which gave us much pleasure. For example, in the course of a debate on foreign affairs in the Indian Parliament Prime Minister Nehru said: 'I would like to draw attention to the task which has been carried out by the UN Observer Corps in Lebanon, because in my opinion they have done an outstanding piece of work, and it is them whom we principally thank that a tragedy has been successfully avoided.'

The last observers were out of Lebanon by 10 December, 1958.

*   *   *

As I said at the outset, UN's role in Lebanon was unique in the organization's history. It may therefore be useful to summarize some of the conclusions I drew from this peace-keeping exercise.

Very probably UNOGIL would have been able to bring the situation under control had it not been for the Iraq coup on 14 July. It is no doubt arguable that in the long run the American landings, combined with Britain's intervention in Jordan, proved a stabilizing factor in the area, but all the same I cannot help recalling the remark Admiral Holloway made to me shortly before his departure: 'That man (Chamoun) had the impertinence to call in American armed forces to protect his own personal interests!'*

It is impossible to overemphasize the part which Dag Hammarskjöld played in the crisis. During the Suez crisis two years earlier it had been fortunate for him that both the superpowers, the USA and the Soviet Union, were more or less on the same side; but this time they were opposed to each other, particularly after the American landings. The problems confronting him were enormous, but he handled them with a wisdom and firmness which impressed everybody. 'Leave it to Dag' became the common refrain. Unfortunately eventually too much was left to Dag and the burden became too heavy for even him to bear.

That co-operation between the three members of the group, with their greatly dissimilar backgrounds, was so smooth and effective, is both remarkable and encouraging. So too was the co-operation between observers from twenty-one different countries. My second-in-command was an Irish Colonel, I. MacCarthy, later to be killed in the Congo. As adjutant I had for a time an officer from Burma, and he was succeeded by

---

* Chamoun has continued to play a leading part in Lebanese politics. He kept a cool head in 1958, and when an attempt was made on his life some years later. Whatever else may be said about him nobody can doubt his courage.

another from Afghanistan. I had a French secretary from the UN Secretariat. I deliberately mixed nationalities as much as possible during the operation.

Some of the officers in my command had already taken part in other UN operations, in Korea, Kashmir, the Middle East, and elsewhere. One of the things we learned in Lebanon was that those with previous UN experience tended to become stale, whereas the newcomers improved as time went on. My own recommendation is that countries which are asked to contribute personnel to UN operations should always be careful to select only men with the highest qualifications. Anyone activated purely by a spirit of adventure should be avoided; even a small minority of unsuitable officers can cause a great deal of trouble for everybody else.

From my own point of view the Lebanese crisis presented both a professional challenge and an exciting experience. But, with all its responsibility, it was an exacting episode and it was a relief to get back to a more or less anonymous existence in Norway. I found, however, on my return that my interest in foreign affairs, and in particular in the problems of the Middle East and of the whole developing world, had greatly increased. I had discovered, too, how inaccurate on the whole was the picture of this particular crisis, of which I had first-hand knowledge, in the international Press and communications media. In future I was to look much more critically at the reports of events of the Middle East appearing in most publications; a truer picture of what was going on and what was behind the events could be found, but it had to be searched for. Not many people have the time, or are prepared to take the trouble, to do this.

My final reflection concerned the enormous significance of the role the UN has to play in the modern world. In spite of all its weaknesses and shortcomings it is the only basis for peaceful coexistence between nations. The outlook for the world, were it not there, would be too tragic to contemplate.

As I was revising the English edition of this book, at the end of 1975, Lebanon was once again in the throes of a civil war, though a much bloodier one than that of which I had been an observer in 1958. As soon as I returned to the Middle East in

1963 warning signals began to be received that such an outbreak was likely within the next ten or fifteen years, and I had
had the feeling that a new crisis was building up. There were
many rumours of arms being imported by various sections of
the population, and it is obvious that outside interference has
played a large part in this latest tragedy, as it did in 1958.

The basic cause of the Lebanese crisis is social injustice with
a religious overtone. In Lebanon an estimated four per cent of
the population is, by any standard, extremely wealthy and lives
in great luxury. But only a few members of this privileged
minority have shown any social conscience, while a large
proportion of the population, particularly that in or near the
main cities, continues to live in great poverty, with little or no
hope or security.

The Lebanese constitution of 1926, with its later amend-
ments, ensured certain privileges for the Christian communities. These privileges were based on a census made at the
beginning of the 1930s, which showed a Christian majority in
the country, and were thought necessary in order to protect a
Christian community in a predominantly Moslem area. With
this privileged position went political power and wealth—
though it must be admitted that very wealthy families are also
to be found among the Moslems and Druzes. Today it is
estimated that not more than forty per cent of the population
is Christian, but no new census has been carried out, because
of Christian fears of what it might reveal.

It appears that this time the extreme Falange organization
has been fighting fanatically to maintain the Christian position. In 1958 the leaders of the Christian communities largely
kept out of the struggle. I sincerely hope that their present-day
successors will be wise enough to follow their example. If they
do not, a full-scale religious war might well follow, with un-
predictable results for the whole area. There is a real danger
that Lebanon could disintegrate as a country, and that this
could provoke a new Middle Eastern explosion.

The Falangists have apparently been trying to frighten the
poorer members of the Christian community with what is
represented as the Moslem threat. But the poor of all communities seem to regard the Palestine Liberation Organization

(PLO) as a revolutionary movement which may offer them the only way of escape from their miseries. This is the main reason for the widespread sympathy for the Palestinians reportedly felt by the bulk of the population.

Hitherto most of the Lebanese political leaders have been unwilling to introduce political and social reforms of any significance. There is, however, a minority which includes moderate people from all the religious communities which understands the problem, but unfortunately they have not been listened to. The former President, Fuad Chehab, was outstanding among those who showed a grasp of the situation.

Reforms must come if Lebanon is to survive. Obviously too, outside interference must cease, and the Lebanese people be left alone to rebuild their country. This rebuilding process must include the formation of a national defence force for the protection of the frontiers, and a police force for internal security. The existing defence and police forces have proved totally inadequate.

There can never be any real internal security without an arms control law. During the 1958 crisis we were much concerned by the lack of any control. Almost every citizen seemed to own at least one weapon. We discussed the problem with a number of Lebanese leaders, urging the need for some legal control over ownership and for a register of all weapons. Unfortunately we never managed to convince them.

In a way the Lebanese crisis is a microcosm of the world's crisis—a confrontation between wealth and poverty, between abundance and hunger.

I have often been struck by the ease with which people nowadays can forget even the most dramatic events. For a few days they follow with bated breath the headlines in the newspapers and the scenes on their television screens, but within a few days some new excitement has taken over and nothing is remembered of the old one.

So it was with the Lebanese affair. By the time I arrived home at Christmas, 1958, the crisis was more or less forgotten, and today only those who had a direct part in it can recollect it at all. All the same, I feel that an account of it has a proper place in this book, because it illustrates how the UN can intervene successfully in a situation which, without it, would probably have been incapable of a peaceful solution.

*   *   *

There is one footnote to the Lebanese operation which should be mentioned here. On 7 October, 1958, I got a telegram from Ralph Bunche, and this time it was the British who were in need of help. It will be recalled that the Iraq coup had provided Chamoun with a welcome excuse to call for help from the Americans. It also provided King Hussein of Jordan and his Government, who felt themselves in imminent danger from Nasser and the newly created UAR, with an excuse to call on Britain for military assistance. Their appeal was heard, and British troops were flown to Jordan, the planes being permitted to fly through Israeli air space. The future of this operation was another of the subjects which came before the special session of the General Assembly in August, and it was agreed that the troops should be withdrawn as soon as the situation had been sufficiently normalized. Their evacuation should be by plane to Cyprus (which was still British territory) and over Arab and not Israeli air space. But this would mean flying over Syria as well as Lebanon, and not only was Syria now a part of the UAR and so part of the State by which King Hussein felt directly threatened, but it, like Egypt, was a country with which Britain had had no diplomatic relations since the Suez War in 1956. So Britain turned to the Secretary-General for help in finding a way out of the impasse.

Bunche in his telegram asked me whether I, with my Air Force experience, could think of a solution. If necessary I could be released temporarily from my UNOGIL duties to carry out this new assignment. He mentioned that President Nasser had agreed in principle to British flights over Syrian air space.

Stated thus, the problem sounds quite a simple one. However, one does not need any lengthy experience of international crises to appreciate that agreement in principle is usually very far from being the end of the story. So I told Bunche that I was prepared to take on the task, and added that there were officers in UNOGIL with suitable flying qualifications whom I could get to assist me. As I saw it our task would be three-fold: 1. To set up the necessary organization; 2. To work out a plan for the operation acceptable to both parties; 3. To exercise control over all planes during the actual flights between Amman and Cyprus.

On 14 October I received instructions from Bunche to go ahead with the preliminary planning. The proposal was that evacuation should begin on 25 October and be completed by 29 October. This meant that all necessary arrangements would have to be made without any delay. I was duly released from UNOGIL, appointed special representative of the Secretary-General, and had the resources of UNTSO in Jerusalem placed at my disposal. My first step was to fly to Cyprus to discover what ideas the British had on how the operation should be mounted. There I met Air-Commodore Weir of the Middle East Air Force Headquarters, who was in favour of the more or less direct route from Amman to Nicosia via Baniyas in South-West Syria. However, this had to be ruled out because it would involve flying close to the armistic demarcation line between Syria and Israel, where flying was not permitted. There was also the problem of what might happen if a plane strayed slightly off its course into Israeli air space. It was now autumn and weather conditions were not always reliable.

From Cyprus I flew to Jerusalem where I met the Chief of Staff of UNTSO, General Von Horn. I asked him to brief the Israeli authorities so that they might know what was going on. The same day I went on to Amman, where I met the Prime Minister, Samir Rifai. His main concern was to get the British out of the country as quickly as possible, but he agreed with me that the direct route favoured by the British would not be acceptable to the UAR. The Chief of Staff of the Jordanian Army was of the same opinion.

At the airport in Amman, which was the Headquarters of the British Forces in Jordan, I met their Commander, Briga-dier T. Pearson of the 16th Independent Parachute Brigade. From there I flew to Damascus where the Chief of the Northern Air Command (later Commander of the Syrian Air Force), General Wadi Moukabari, confirmed that the British proposal was unacceptable. He suggested an alternative route, running roughly east from Amman to Shahba in Syria, then north to Saassa, and so to Saida in Lebanon. That sounded reasonable. The first British reaction was unfavourable, but on second thoughts they realized that there was no other real alternative.

Now it was time to move on to detailed planning, and it soon became obvious that you can come up against reefs in the air as well as in the sea. The Syrians insisted that the planes should fly in groups of three, but the British protested that their pilots had no training in formation flying, which could make it dangerous, particularly if the weather was bad. The Syrians yielded on this point, but insisted that all flights should be in daylight and that there should be only a limited number of British planes over Syria at any one time.

The British argued that for navigational purposes they would have to have a radio beacon at Shahba. So we borrowed one from them and manned it with two radio technicians loaned by UNTSO in Jerusalem. Both, as it happened, were Norwegians, Ivar Saatvedt and John Böe. When it first came into their hands the beacon did not work, but they managed to repair it, and it functioned perfectly throughout the airlift.

At a meeting with Moukabari on 23 October these plans were accepted in principle, and the next morning, at 1020 hours, they were signed. There were to be two trial flights that day from Cyprus to Amman, and the planes were due to cross the Syrian border at 1030 hours, so that there had been no time to lose, and when, immediately after the signing, Moukabari checked with Damascus flight control, he learned that the planes were already on their way. Later the same day there was a ceremony at Beirut airport at which the British signed.

The next day, 25 October, the airlift began. The operation was carried out by sixteen men from seven countries, and consisted of twelve pilots, a signals officer, a cipher officer, and two radio technicians. My second in command was Lt-Colonel Westerberg from Sweden. We had at our disposal our own signals network, the radio beacon, and one Dakota plane. The pilots were stationed in the control towers at the airports in Damascus, Amman, Beirut, and Nicosia. Thanks to the outstanding co-operation of everyone concerned, not least the Syrians, the operation passed off without a hitch. I took up my own position in Damascus and was able to note on several occasions how the Syrian air control guided the British pilots on to their correct path. The evacuation was completed according to plan on 29 October without complications of any description. It accounted for 2,168 men, 117 vehicles, 85 trailers, and 74 airborne trailers, 25 guns, 230,500 lbs of stores. These were carried in 86 flights. In addition six fighter aircraft and three transports of the RAF, which had been in Jordan, were flown out. A very minor incident in world history, no doubt, and one that has been completely forgotten; but all the same the sort of incident which could not have been success- fully concluded if the UN, with all its political and diplomatic expertise, had not been there to handle it.

CHAPTER 2

A CAREER IN THE AIR

❊ ❊ ❊ ❊

When in 1958 I received to my great surprise the invitation
from the Secretary-General of UN to go to Lebanon I had for
two years been AOC in South Norway. But when I look back
on a career which has taken me, as Chief of Air Staff, to the
top of my profession. I cannot help remarking how free I feel
myself to have been from the romanticism which so many of
my contemporaries seem to have felt for flying. Of course I
had, I suppose, like everybody else of my generation heard
about the legendary achievements of Amundsen and those
pioneers of polar flight, Riisen-Larsen, Dietrichson, Balchen,
Omdahl and others, not to mention Trygve Gran, who, almost
unnoticed, made the first flight across the North Sea in 1914.
And then there was Lindbergh's solo Atlantic flight, the most
dramatic of all. But never in these early years did it occur to
me that flying was to be my life.

No member of my family before me had made any of the
Services his profession. Most of them had been sailors, as skip-
pers or owners of ships. At the same time they had been
merchants and farmers in the districts of Melsomvik and Tönsberg. The patriarch of the family, Jacob Bull, had come to
Norway from Angelen in Schleswig in 1700 as Captain of his
own ship, and settled down in Tönsberg, where he prospered
both as captain and ship-owner, and soon became a leading
citizen. He married Martha Örbech, they had sixteen sons and
three daughters—a large family even in those days. In 1733
he had the unusual honour of presenting twelve of his sons to
King Christian VI when that monarch visited his Jarlsberg
estates.

One of these sons, Peter, was born in 1709 and married Elizabeth Marcusdatter Faye. Tradition records that the Faye family came to Norway from France during the persecution of the Huguenots, and Elizabeth's grandfather, Marcus Faye, is said to have crossed the North Sea from the Orkneys to Bergen in the winter of 1641/2. Almost exactly 300 years later I myself, his descendant, found myself in a form of exile in those same islands, but in a more fortunate position than he, since I was commanding a Norwegian fighter squadron.

Our family's close connection with the sea was broken in 1900 when health compelled my grandfather to give it up. So it was that my father, Gjert Bull, became the family's first land crab. In 1885 he began working with his uncle, Conrad Langaard, who eventually built up Norway's biggest tobacco factory. My father became, while still comparatively young, manager of the factory. He used to work long hours. He would complete the same hours as the factory hands, come home to dinner, and then go back to the factory for a further three or four hours. I seldom saw him except on Sundays. His special skill was in the purchasing of raw tobacco, which involved a lot of travelling. In 1914 he decided to leave the tobacco firm and set up his own Agency business, which prospered until the difficult years immediately following the First World War.

We lived in Oslo at Uranienborg Terrace, where we had moved three years after my birth on 28 June, 1907. Uranienborg Terrace was regarded as one of the 'better' streets to live in; it was, in any case, a delightful place for children since there was virtually no traffic in the neighbourhood. I can look back on a happy childhood. Our parents were reasonably well off and I went to Vestheim School, where I stayed for 12 years until my leaving examination in 1925. The headmaster, O. J. Skattum, was a man of outstanding ability, who taught us that freedom and responsibility must go together.

I was dissatisfied with the results of my final examination, since I had done badly in mathematics which was supposed to be my best subject. So I decided to try for a year at the Military Academy. I was accepted, and though my original intention had been to stay there for one year only I enjoyed it so much that I applied for entry to the senior section of the

Academy, where regular officers were trained on a two-year course.

The Armed Forces were not particularly popular in Norway at this time. People remembered the so-called 'broken rifles' events when troops had been called in to deal with a general strike. Some of my colleagues in the Academy hesitated to show themselves in public in uniform because of the reception they got. This never worried me much. I liked the contact with other people, the open air life and the hard training.

At that time was was no residential accommodation at the Academy. This did not matter so much to those of us who lived in Oslo, but it was hard for the others. In an effort, I suppose, to be democratic, officers and cadets used to eat together, but the cadets were served poorer rations. I remember well the thin milk, coffee, bread and margarine for breakfast. The dinner was hardly any better. We had to supplement our rations with parcels from home and visits to the canteen. We worked hard, from seven in the morning till late at night, with only an hour off for lunch, and though this kept us fit it kept us hungry too.

All in all, my time at the Academy was well spent, and in 1928 I emerged as a 'supernumerary unpaid First Lieutenant in the Fourth Infantry Division'. During these years my interest in flying had increased, and I decided to put in for the Army Flying School, as it was then called. In August, 1929, I heard that my application had been accepted.

The Flying School was at Kjeller, and the training planes then in use were of a type manufactured in Norway called Kaje. This was a 2-seater biplane, the pupil sitting in front with the instructor behind him, and the only safety precaution was a belt around the pupil's waist. There were ten of us under instruction. I do not know how a pupil at a Flying School feels about it today—perhaps he sees it all as purely a technical problem. But in those days it was all exciting and dramatic. Oddly enough I cannot remember anything in particular about my first solo flight, though I have a vivid recollection of my second. The rule was that on your first solo you had to carry a sandbag in the rear seat, but that on the second you could take a passenger. I asked a Ditlev Smith, later to become a civilian pilot and be killed in 1936 in an accident, to come up with me. He agreed, but no sooner had we taken off than I saw him climb out of his seat and on to one of the wings. There was no particular reason for his action: he did it, he said, 'just for fun'. I was not amused.

There was seldom any serious accident involving these planes, thanks largely to their low speeds (the Kaje's cruising speed was about 120km an hour). But sooner or later something is bound to happen, and I was not to be allowed to escape completely. We were on winter manoeuvres at Mesnalia. The weather was bad, and contrary to regulations I turned at low speed, lost height, and crash-landed on the frozen Lake Mesna. Luckily it was covered with fairly thick snow and I suffered nothing worse than two black eyes. Forty years later in Jerusalem I picked a piece of glass about 3 mm long out from under my eyebrows with a pair of tweezers. It came from my broken goggles.

My training lasted a year, and in 1931 I was back at Kjeller, but it was now I who was in the instructor's seat. Like most young Norwegians at this time I was, I suppose, not particularly interested in politics, at any rate in foreign politics, though we gained some experience of other countries and people when we were sent on courses abroad or met foreigners attending our own courses. The winter Infantry School was very popular, and in 1931 I was selected for its course at Geilo. There were many foreign officers on this course, one of whom was a German called Eduard Dietl. He was an expert skier from, as far as I can remember, an Alpine Regiment (skiing naturally played a prominent part in the course), and as a man he was pleasant, informal, and with a good sense of humour. As an officer he was outstanding, for his whole attitude was much more aggressive than that of us Norwegians. It turned out that he was someone we were to hear more of. In 1940 he turned up as a General and Commander of the German forces attacking Narvik. Later he had command of the 20th Army Group, the so-called Lapland Army, which fought on the northern Finnish front. He was killed at the end of the war in a flying accident on his way back from a visit to Hitler's Headquarters.

It was in the following years, with the rise of Nazism in Germany, that the Norwegian public and politicians began to grow more conscious of what was brewing in the outside world. But, though budget allocations for defence were increased, the Norwegian Air Force was still operating under many handicaps. There were problems of organization: the Army and Navy each had their own planes, and though a committee recommended the creation of an integrated air defence system this was not acted upon. Then there was the question of the type of planes in service. We had 30 or 40 old (1927) Fokker reconnaissance planes as well as Moth trainers, but what we needed were fighter planes. It was decided that some more should be purchased, but a condition was made that the aircraft should be fitted with a special engine, called the Panther, which was manufactured on licence in Norway. We tried to fit these engines into British planes and into Swedish planes, but with no success. Eventually the politicians realized that this approach was no good. The clause in the contract which insisted on the use of Panther engines was dropped, and I was myself a member of a group of three sent to Britain to test out aircraft for possible purchase. Our recommendation was that we should take the Gloucester Gladiator, but by then several years had been wasted.

There had been a good many German officers besides Dietl on courses in Norway, and as a gesture of reciprocity I was, in the autumn of 1937, seconded for duties with the German Air Force—though I had to pay all my expenses, including my travel, out of my own pocket. My first stopping place was Dortmund, and later I went on to Schwerin in Mecklenburg. I was naturally impressed by the size and quality of the German Air Force, and with many of the pilots I became good friends. I was allowed to fly all the planes I wanted and to ask any technical details about them I liked, but we never discussed politics. All the same there were several small facts which I could not help noticing. For example, I was for a time attached to a squadron whose Commanding Officer was a certain Captain Palm. He was badly burned about the face and, though I cannot recall anyone telling me this in so many words, I gained the firm impression that he had been shot down while serving on the Nationalist side in Spain. When I left the squadron he said, 'Come back in two years' time and I'll show you something really surprising.' That would have been in 1939.

When war did in fact break out in September, 1939, the Norwegian Air Force and Navy were mobilized and I found myself on the staff of the Army Air Force. I felt certain that Norway would sooner or later be drawn into the war, and during the following months great efforts were made to strengthen both the military and naval air forces. Over a hundred planes—Curtis, Douglas, Caproni, Northrop, and six Heinkel—were ordered, but by the time the war caught up with us none of them, except the Heinkels, had actually been delivered.

On Monday, 8 April, we heard of the British mine-laying operation in Norwegian coastal waters off Möre. The same evening I had been invited for a formal dinner party at the home of the German Air Attaché, Captain Spiller. I rang the authorities to ask whether I should go and they said I should —we were still friends with Germany. So I went. There was only one other non-German there, Captain Erik Anker Steen, Director of Naval Intelligence. The atmosphere during dinner was understandably tense, and several times Spiller was called to the telephone to speak with Berlin. At about midnight Steen went home. I stayed on for a quarter of an hour or so and then left. I had scarcely entered my front door when the first air raid sounded. I quickly changed from dinner jacket to uniform and drove down to my office at Akerhus. The duty officer could tell me nothing about what was happening; nor could the general staff or the Admiralty. After a great deal of telephoning I came to the conclusion that not a single responsible person in the whole of the Norwegian armed forces had any idea what was going on.

According to the operational plan our wartime headquarters were to be in a small hotel at Vettakollåsen, in the hills outside Oslo. We moved out there, and I then rang up the family of Captain Motzfeldt, who was on a purchasing mission for aircraft in the States. His home was near Fornebu, where there was an aerodrome, and it was his wife who answered the 'phone. I told her that the situation was extremely serious and advised her to get out of town as quickly as possible. She told me that German planes had already landed at Fornebu. So the first information I had of the German landings was from a young housewife preoccupied with looking after her infant twins—one of whom, Ulrik, was my godson.

The fighter squadron stationed at Fornebu gave a good account of itself, shooting down at least four, more probably six, German planes before its own planes were put out of action by being obliged to land on frozen lakes where fresh supplies of fuel and ammunition could not reach them. Other Air Force planes in Southern Norway suffered the same fate.

The story of the next few weeks is too well known for there to be any need for me to tell it again. It was nearly a month later, on a dark and tempestuous night, that of 6 May, that I found myself with other Air Force officers in a fishing boat off Alesund. Resistance in Southern Norway was by now at an end, but orders had been given that as many pilots as possible should make their way to Britain to obtain new aircraft with which to continue the war in Northern Norway. Two days later, on 8 May, in cloudy weather, we sighted some warships not far off. We signalled to them with a pocket torch and a British destroyer came alongside. They asked us who we were and where we were going. We found that we had overshot our target, which was the Shetland Islands, but after borrowing a compass from the destroyer we corrected our course, and the next day sailed into Lerwick harbour. A new phase of the war had begun for us.

Our first idea was to get the planes ordered in the States by the Norwegian Government to Britain and to establish Norwegian squadrons there. But no suitable airfields were available for us in Britain, and France seemed more promising, though by the time our advance party had gone there France too was on the point of collapse and had to be ruled out. We then received fom the Canadian Government the offer of Toronto Island Airport as a training centre, and this was accepted. I was one of four officers sent over as an advance party to Toronto, the main party arriving at the beginning of August. We numbered 120 in all, officers and men.

To begin with the Canadians were somewhat sceptical as to our value. The world's Press was full of that new and opprobrious title which had its origins in Norway—Quisling— and this did a great deal of harm to the reputation of Norway as a nation. But after a while the Canadians appreciated that we meant business and were determined to fight for our country, whereupon their attitude changed. They were to prove themselves the most helpful and pleasant people it has ever been my lot to mix with, and I came to look on Canada as my second home.

At last the unified Air Force, the need for which had long been obvious to everybody, came into existence, being first realized in Toronto in December, 1940. News of the training camp, nicknamed 'Little Norway', spread round the world wherever Norwegians were to be found, and soon volunteers were arriving there from all quarters. And not only Norwegians, for many Danes, anxious to serve, came too.

One day one of the doctors told me of a recruit who was anxious to join the flying school. His name was Olai Grön-mark; he was 32 years old, and only had an elementary education. He had lived in Canada for many years, working in the mines. In spite of the fact that usually we insisted that recruits for flying duties should be under 25 and have a school leaving certificate the doctor was insistent that we should try to make an exception in this case. 'He has many excellent qualities,' he said, 'a terrific physique and the real fighting spirit. Do try him!' So Grönmark was accepted, and all went well. Just before Christmas—in fact, I think on Christmas Eve—he was due to fly solo. He started with the brakes partly on, failed to take off, and landed on Lake Ontario, luckily in shallow water. An extremely unhappy pupil climbed out of the cockpit. He was convinced that he would be failed, but he was given another chance, eventually passed out, and was sent to England. It was discovered that he was too tall and too broad in the shoulders for a Spitfire, so he was attached to an English squadron of B-25 Mitchell light bombers, where he would have plenty of elbow-room. He proved an outstanding pilot, and ended the war a Major, many times decorated. After the war Grönmark remained in Norway and in the Air Force, dying a few years ago—a fine officer who did good service to his country in peace and war. His attitude was typical of that of many of our pilots.

There was an urgent need for training planes and by the beginning of September we managed to acquire some Fairchild PT19s. These proved very good, but came with no flying manuals or instruction books, and the Canadian Air Force had none to spare. But happening one day to be in a Toronto bookshop I saw a book called *Teach Yourself to Fly in Ten Lessons*. I bought all the available copies and they came in useful.

Back in Britain I was attached to Squadron 242 at North Weald, outside London, which was engaged at that time in fighter sweeps over Northern France and on bomber escort for attacks on targets on the French coast. At the end of July, 1941, I was one of those concerned in the formation of the first all-Norwegian fighter unit. This was based at Catterick and equipped with Hurricane Mark 1s, which were already worn out by the service they had put in during the Battle of Britain and elsewhere. Almost every day we had difficulty with them and there were several emergency landings. The RAF suspected the trouble was due to our technical incompetence and set up a Commission of Inquiry. This reported in our favour and as a result we were issued with brand new Hurricane Mark 2s. In August we moved to Castletown airfield in the northern tip of Scotland, and later to Skeabrae in the Orkneys, where we had the special task of defending the naval base at Scapa Flow. Two planes were stationed in the Shetlands. The old ties between the Islands and Norway ensured us a warm welcome.

It was then my lot to cross the Atlantic again to become Camp Commandant and OC Training Section at 'Little Norway', but I was back on flying duties in Britain in time for D-Day, attached to Second Tactical Air Force, Squadron 107, flying Mosquitoes. The liberation of Norway took place on 8 May 1945, and on Whit Sunday, 20 May, I flew in, crossing the coast at Lista and landing at Gardenmoen airfield.

After the first excitement of victory came the reckoning. During the war 750 young Norwegians had succeeded in join-

36

ing the Air Force. Of these 278 were killed, 203 in battle and 75 in training or other accidents. In other words more than one in three had lost their lives, and in addition we had to count those who had been taken prisoner or wounded. But though the cost was high it was well worth paying. Norwegian squadrons won the reputation of being second to none among the allies, and it was thanks to the new spirit engendered by the wartime struggle that we emerged a rejuvenated nation.

I remained in the Air Force after the war was over, serving first as head of one of the four regional commands (Tröndelag) into which Norway was divided, and then at headquarters in Oslo as head of the organization section, and then as Chief of Staff to the Commander of the Air Force. Two years after my return from Lebanon I was appointed Chief of Air Staff.

CHAPTER 3

DEMARCATION DISPUTES

✽ ✽ ✽ ✽

On 31 January, 1963, I received a letter from Norway's Ambassador to the UN, Sivert Nielsen, a distinguished diplomat, the contents of which came as a considerable surprise. 'Ralph Bunche,' he wrote, 'has asked me to make tactful enquiries whether you might possibly be interested in taking over the post of Head of the United Nations Truce Supervision Organization in the Middle East (UNTSO) when Von Horn retires, as is expected, some time in the spring, probably April. If you are interested, and if you can be released from your present duties, the Secretary-General would get in touch with your Government.' Nielsen strongly recommended me to accept the post. Both the Minister of Defence, Gudmund Harlem, and the Chief of Defence Staff, General Bjarne Öen, whom I consulted, were equally in favour, and so within a week I had notified New York of my acceptance.

Not everybody I spoke to thought I had chosen rightly. Trygve Lie, whom I met several times that spring, warned me against taking on the job. I gathered from what he said that his views on the Middle East situation had been considerably modified; starting out, when he became UN's first Secretary-General, as a fervent supporter of Zionism and later of Israel, he had now come to the conclusion that the Palestine Arabs had never been given a fair deal.

A month later Sivert Nielsen wrote again. Bunche was delighted that I am willing to serve and U Thant had also expressed his satisfaction. He had been in touch with the Governments concerned—the Arab States and Israel—as well as with the permanent members of the Security Council and

38

they had all signified their approval. He suggested 1 June as the date for me to take over. I was particularly interested to learn of the favourable response from the Arabs. I doubt whether they would have accepted any officer from a NATO country had they not come to know me personally during my time in Lebanon, and when I had negotiated directly with the Governments of Syria and Jordan over the evacuation of British troops from Jordan. I had served a useful apprenticeship. Unfortunately, during U Thant's soundings, the news of my prospective appointment had leaked out. There were many governments which would have liked the post for one of their nationals. The Americans, for example, were eager to put forward the name of one of their most distinguished commanders from the Second World War for it—though it is hard to imagine that they can really have thought that an American would at that time have been acceptable to the Arabs.

On 2 April I received an official invitation from U Thant to become head of UNTSO with the rank of Under Secretary-General, which meant that I would be directly responsible to him, though in day-to-day affairs my dealings would be with Bunche. At the same time he asked me to come to New York for consultations. I left Norway on 17 May. Next day I had a long discussion with the Secretary-General and Bunche about general conditions in the Middle East. It was my first meeting with U Thant and I formed a very favourable impression of him. He had much of the wisdom which we westerners too often lack. He has been accused of a lack of dynamism, but his calm diplomacy was a great deal preferable to the energetic intervention of a less prudent man. In the course of the next few years my admiration for U Thant was if anything to increase rather than lessen. At this meeting Bunche expressed concern at recent developments in the Middle East, particularly at the implications of the Israeli Government's plans to divert water from the River Jordan for irrigation purposes in Southern Israel. This was due to start in the summer of 1964.

After four days in New York I flew back to Oslo. The plan was that I should go out to the area at once, meeting my predecessor, General Von Horn, in Beirut, and that my family should join me in the autumn. Von Horn was an extremely able officer, but his somewhat hasty temper had brought him into conflict with the Israeli Government and it was thought best that it should not be left for him to introduce his successor. I arrived in Beirut on 26 May and was met by Von Horn's 'Senior Observer', the American Colonel Bob Churley. Von Horn had himself been diverted to take charge of the UN's operations in Yemen, but he sent me a letter, which was not altogether cheering: 'Welcome!' he wrote. 'I wish you the best of luck in your job. It is impossible and thankless, but very fascinating.'

What in fact was this job I was taking on? What was UNTSO? The United Nations Truce Supervision Organization had its origin in the Security Council resolution of 23 April, 1948, which provided for the setting up of an organization to supervise the armistice. During the first phase of its existence (1948-9) UNTSO's main task was to maintain observation over coasts, harbours, airports, borders, strategic road crossings, and ceasefire lines to ensure that none of the combatants obtained reinforcements of weapons or personnel.

During the second phase (1949-56) UNTSO's mission was to supervise the ceasefire which had been ordered by the Security Council on 15 July, 1948, and confirmed on 11 August, 1949. It was also supposed to ensure respect for the armistice agreements which had been arranged under UN supervision between Israel and her four Arab neighbours—Egypt, Jordan, Syria and Lebanon. These agreements provided for four Mixed Armistice Commissions (MACs), one for each of the adjoining States which had been at war with Israel, consisting of personnel from the signatory States under the chairmanship of a UN representative. The MACs were subsidiaries of UNTSO.

The third phase (1956-67) covered the period between the Suez War and the June War. After Suez Israel claimed that her armistice agreement with Egypt had lapsed. There was no support at the UN for this point of view, but as Israel refused to take part in meetings of the Israel-Egypt MAC there was nothing much that could be done about it. UN forces (UNEF) were by now in position along the Egyptian side of the armistice line between Egypt and Israel and they took over the

MAC's task of observation and reporting. If a complaint was sent to the MAC it had to be considered without Israeli participation, but all the same the system went on working fairly well until the June 1967 War.

The fourth phase (1967–73) covered the period between the June War and the Yom Kippur or Ramadan War. After June, 1967, Israel ceased to recognize any of the other three armistice agreements (those with Jordan, Syria, and Lebanon), but neither the UN nor the Arab Governments accepted this act of unilateral abrogation. In this phase it became UNTSO's main task to supervise the 1967 ceasefire lines between Israel and Syria and the ceasefire sector along the Suez Canal. In theory all the armistice agreements of 1949 continued in being, but in practise this did not amount to much. Whenever there was a violation of one of the agreements during the second and third phases the first step was always to try to remove the cause of the violation. Once a ceasefire had been restored there would be a further investigation by the MAC concerned —that is to say by UNTSO observers. This could take ten or more days. Then as a rule the observers' report would be discussed in the MAC, one or both sides would put forward a resolution, and unless the chairman was successful in resolving the dispute himself this resolution would be voted on. Really serious breaches of the armistice would be brought before the Security Council. ISMAC (the Israel–Syria MAC) was a special case, since no joint meetings of it had in fact been held since 1951. Complaints which would normally have come before it were forwarded by it to the Secretary-General of UN and by him, if they seemed sufficiently serious, to the Security Council. But during the fourth phase all ceasefire violations had to be reported direct to the Secretary-General who immediately informed the Security Council. This meant of course it was essential that the observers' reports should be absolutely correct, and it was in this phase too that the time factor played a vital part.

Generally speaking it can be safely said that UNTSO functioned satisfactorily when it was a question of re-establishing the ceasefire after a violation—apart of course from the occasions in 1956 and 1967 when violations escalated into war. But after the spring of 1969, when there was to all intents and purposes a war of attrition between Israel and Egypt, UNTSO could exercise little influence on either party. We were then obliged to become observers of a war rather than a ceasefire.

After spending a few days in Beirut I flew to Jerusalem on 2 June, 1963, landing at Kolandia airport in the Jordanian West Bank, north of the city. There followed a series of visits aimed at gaining a first-hand knowledge of the attitudes of both sides. Israel came first on my list. I had a number of talks at the Foreign Ministry, was granted an audience by the President (Ben-Zvi), and discussed the situation with the Prime Minister, David Ben-Gurion. I also had a useful meeting with the Foreign Minister, Golda Meir. She told me that recently she had been in the Negev with her daughter, where they had watched people drilling for water. Her daughter had said, 'I hope for God's sake we find water, not oil.' She quoted this as an illustration of how precious water was for Israel. Golda Meir added, 'Oil we can buy; water we cannot live without.'

Golda Meir struck me as a very impressive and persuasive personality, though she has shown little or no understanding for the Arabs of Palestine or for the justice of their demands. She has always talked a great deal about the 'historical and spiritual rights of the Jews', but it is difficult to accept the validity of 'historic rights' which can only be achieved at the expense of people who have been living in the same place for 2,000 years. The principle which she applies on behalf of the Jews, and by which she justifies the expulsion of the Palestinians, would, if applied elsewhere, reduce the world to a state of total chaos. As far as 'spiritual rights' go there can be no doubt that the Jews have strong claims, particularly in regard to Jerusalem. But they are not alone in this. So have the Christians, for Jerusalem is the cradle of Christianity. So have the Moslems. The resolution passed by the General Assembly in 1947 which called for the internationalization of Jerusalem was fully justified, even though today it may not appear to be practical politics.

Jerusalem is the most fascinating city I know. My family and I lived in the former Government House, seat of the

British High Commissioner in mandatory days and after 1949 the headquarters of UNTSO. It has a magnificent view over the mountains of Judaea, Mount Scopus, the Mount of Olives, the Dead Sea, the Mountains of Moab and the whole panorama of Jerusalem itself, old and new.

In former times Jerusalem was a place where there was a great degree of mutual understanding between followers of the three great monotheistic religions. Here they lived side by side and learned to respect each other. Jerusalem has been called the city of peace, though its history perhaps does not justify this title. But if it is indeed ever to become a city of peace—and, as it should be, to become a place where people of all religions can meet for prayer, meditation, study and research—its foundations will have to be based on justice and not falsehood. This means that the Arabs will have to regain that part of the City which was theirs until 1967 and that the whole City must be a place where Arabs and Jews can come together in confidence and understanding. Were this to happen in one place, it is conceivable that understanding might spread further, and that in this way Jerusalem might become the seed from which a general reconciliation between Arabs and Jews would grow.

From Jerusalem I flew to the Arab capitals. In Cairo I saw the Foreign Minister, Mahmoud Fawzi, and in Damascus the Prime Minister and Foreign Minister, Salah Bitar. In Beirut I had an audience with my old colleague and friend of five years before, President Fuad Chehab, and with the Prime Minister, Rashid Karami. In Amman I had an audience with King Hussein. Wherever I went I found a friendly reception and all seemed well-disposed to UNTSO. I got the impression that, though there might be little sign of any agreement between the parties to the dispute, I had arrived at a fairly peaceful moment. This impression was not to persist for long.

The first serious incident took place only a few days after I arrived in Jerusalem, and was on the border between Israel and Syria. On 9 June, 1963, we were told that the Syrian authorities had filed a complaint to the effect that an Israeli patrol boat had fired on a small village on the eastern shore of Lake Tiberias, and that simultaneously Israeli planes had attacked the village. No planes had been in action in the area since 1951, so that if the Syrian charge was correct this represented a serious escalation of the border fighting.

Our people made a thorough investigation. The air attacks were said to have been made from north to south, and the UN had observation posts both north and south of the area. There were no signs of any bomb damage near the village, so we came to the conclusion that there had in fact been no attack from the air. The shots fired by the patrol boat were presumably in answer to Syrian boats fishing in the lake or to Syrians firing on Israeli fishing boats.

Two days later I called on the Syrian Prime Minister, Salah Bitar, who repeated the accusation that planes had been involved. I told him bluntly that they had not, and that what had happened was that Israeli planes had broken the sound barrier in the area and the bangs had made the local people think bombs were dropping. I said I spoke not simply as head of the Supervision Organization but as an expert on these matters. In fact I expressed myself so emphatically that my political adviser, Henri Vigier, who was with me, became quite uneasy. But my explanation was accepted.

There may on this occasion have been no air activity but there certainly had been exchanges between Israelis and Syrians on the ground. This hostility had a long and complicated background. When the British and French mandates over Palestine and Syria were drawn up the frontier between them was described as lying 30ft east of Lake Tiberias. This meant the people who had lived in villages east of the Lake for perhaps hundreds of years found themselves cut off from their traditional fishing grounds and obliged to ask the British mandatory authorities for permission to fish as usual. When the Israelis occupied the area they claimed that the Syrians had no automatic right to fish in the Lake but would have to ask for, and obtain, permits from the Israeli authorities before they could do so. Since Syria did not recognize Israel this was out of the question, so all fishing by Syria that took place was, strictly speaking, illegal. Israeli patrol boats fired on any Syrian fisherman they came across. In retaliation Syria would fire on Israeli fishing boats.

I took this up with the Israeli authorities, my aim being to reduce the activities of the patrol boats. It seemed to me illogical to expect people who had used these fishing grounds from time immemorial to stop doing so now. But all my representations were in vain; the Israelis insisted that if the Syrians were to be allowed to fish, they must recognize Israeli sovereignty over the lake. One of my predecessors had, with the support of the Secretary-General, suggested that the UN should have a patrol boat on the Lake, but this too was rejected by Israel, although there can be no doubt that such a step would have contributed greatly to the relaxation of tension.

There was continual trouble over the demarcation line at Lake Tiberias between Syria and Israel. On 13 July there was another incident, the repercussions of which continued up to Christmas. Three Israelis and three Belgians had been visiting the village of Ein Gev in the demilitarized zone on the east shore of the Lake where, among other attractions, there was a very good fish restaurant. They set off back home in a small plastic-hulled boat, aiming north towards Capernaum. This was a risky—indeed a foolhardy—proceeding, because in the event of engine failure they could easily be driven onto the northern part of the eastern shore of the Lake by the westerly wind which often blows across the Lake in the latter part of the day. This would create problems, for although the Israelis claimed sovereignty over the whole of the eastern shore it was the Syrians who commanded it militarily. This is exactly what happened. The engine packed up, the boat drifted onto the eastern shore of the Lake north of the demilitarized zone, and its six passengers were arrested by Syrian troops. The three Belgians were released after a couple of weeks, but, although we had an observation post near the place where the boat had come ashore, and so had a witness of all that happened, it was to be a long time before we could secure the release of the three Israelis.

When the Belgians were released they confirmed the account given by our observer at OP Foxtrot, Major Yancy, that the boat had simply drifted on shore because of engine failure. But that was not good enough for the Syrians. They remained suspicious that there must be something more to the incident. It is, of course, this atmosphere of suspicion which pervades the whole Middle Eastern atmosphere and makes the work of any outside agency so difficult. There can be no doubt that the Israeli intelligence service had at all times been highly efficient, and it was perhaps not altogether surprising that the Syrians should think that here was a new and ingenious form of infiltration—even though all those in the boat were wearing nothing but swimming trunks when they were captured.

It was unfortunate that there was only one man in the observation post at the moment when the boat was beached. The Syrians insisted that the observer had given an incorrect account of the affair and declared him *persona non grata*, which meant that we had no alternative but to withdraw him. But this is a fairly complex proceeding, involving the Secretary-General, because he is responsible to the Governments which have put observers at his disposal. Obviously, if an officer has to be sent home it could, even if he is in no way to blame, have an adverse effect on his career. This means that if an officer is declared *persona non grata* the Secretary-General is bound to take an extremely serious view of the case and to demand full supporting evidence from the country making the complaint. Usually, however, the complaint is made in general terms, with no detailed charges, and however hard the Secretary-General pressed for them he seldom got the details he wanted. We came up against this sort of situation on a number of occasions.

So the three Israelis continued to be held by the Syrians who refused to accept our version of what had happened, and meanwhile we were under strong pressure from the Israelis to get their people freed. Meetings and telephone calls went on daily for months. I sent my Legal Adviser and Information Officer to Damascus to try, through friendly intermediaries, to bring pressure on the authorities there, but they had no success. The only thing the Syrians suggested was that there should first be a more general exchange of prisoners and after this the case of the three men in the boat should be considered. At that time the Israelis held ten Syrians, and the Syrians eight Israelis, not counting the latest three. My predecessor had been negotiating for an exchange, but without results. Then more Syrians were picked up after the Lebanese boat, the *St Hilarion*, had been arrested in Israeli territorial waters and four Syrian sailors taken off it. Eventually there were nineteen Syrians and eleven Israelis available for an exchange.

The Israelis were desperately anxious to get their men freed. This was natural enough, though my own feeling is that if their press and propaganda machine had been less violent we might have got results sooner. I had several meetings on the matter with Golda Meir and Abba Eban, who was acting Prime Minister at the time. Our negotiations were so protracted that on 1 October one leading paper, *Lamerhav*, wrote: 'A crisis in relations between the Government and General Bull is to be feared if immediate steps to secure the release of the prisoners are not taken.' This was not particularly encouraging, though I had to admit that the Government representatives themselves never used such threatening language. They knew that I was using all the pressure on Syria I could—the Syrians in fact began to consider I was 'pro-Israel', which did nothing to increase my effectiveness as a negotiator.

By 10 November matters had progressed far enough for us to begin discussing the timing of the exchange, but on 13 November General Amin Hafez seized power in Damascus and that meant more delays. Nevertheless, some days later our plans were complete. All that remained was to work out the form of words which was to be used during the exchange. Each prisoner was to be asked three questions—what was his name; had he received correct treatment while in captivity; and had he recovered all his property. Originally there was to have been a fourth question—did the prisoner want to be repatriated—but after consultation with both sides we decided to drop it. The Syrians in particular were opposed to its inclusion, even though it had originally been put forward by the General Assembly in 1952, because they thought the Israelis would put pressure on their prisoners to say they wanted to stay in Israel, which would have the result of making the exchange one-sided. In the end it was decided that before the exchange took place UN observers should question each prisoner to find out whether he wished to be sent home or not.

47

Two of the Syrians said they did not. One was wanted for murder in Syria, and as he admitted to an observer that he had killed a man he had to be returned. But the other was not exchanged.

The exchange itself took place in the middle of Banat Yacub Bridge over the River Jordan, north of Lake Tiberias on 21 December. Israeli troops took up their position at one end of the bridge and Syrian troops at the other. The agreed questions were put to the prisoners, and then they were simultaneously marched across to the other side. Fortunately news of the exchange was kept secret until after it had been carried out. If there had been any adverse advance comment in the Press one or other of the parties might easily have cancelled it.

After the exchange Golda Meir wrote to the Secretary-General to thank him, Ralph Bunche, myself and Colonel Wilkinson (Chairman of the Israel–Syrian MAC) for their part in securing the release of the eleven Israelis. Later, some of the Israelis who had been released reported that there were still Israelis in captivity in Syria. Syria also reported that Syrians remained captive in Israel, claiming at one time that their number was as high as fifty-one. Even though this particular exercise had been successfully concluded, similar cases continued to occur.

In January, 1964, the prisoner question cropped up again. When I called on General Yitzhak Rabin, who had become Chief of Staff of the Israeli Defence Forces, he asked me if I had any news of remaining Israeli prisoners in Syria. I made enquiries from Damascus, and on 20 February received the answer that Syria had no prisoners for exchange. This was disappointing, but we continued our efforts. Two years later, in August, 1966, we were able to effect another exchange—four Israelis against six Syrians. One of the Israelis involved had been a prisoner for about twelve years. We also managed to arrange an exchange between Egypt and Israel. Some Israeli civilians, engaged in the melon harvest, had crossed the demarcation line at Gaza and been picked up by the UN forces who had handed them over to the Egyptians. After a good deal of difficulty we were able to exchange three Israelis against three Egyptians in March, 1965. One of the Egyptians had been sentenced to eighteen years' imprisonment on charges of espionage.

There were other incidents when people inadvertently crossed the demarcation lines between Israel and Jordan or Syria. These lines were not marked on the ground, and though there were a number of warning notices it was easy for people to make mistakes. UNTSO always had to follow up such cases. If foreigners were involved they were quickly returned, but if Israelis or Syrians were involved the problem was much more complicated.

Lake Tiberias was not the only part of the demarcation line between Syria and Israel to cause us trouble. Many incidents occurred in the demilitarized zone which had been agreed in the armistice (see Appendix number II). The zone was made up of three sectors, with a total area of 66.5 square kilometres—there was a small sector in the extreme north-east corner of what used to be Palestine, a larger triangular-shaped sector south of the former Lake Huleh (now drained), with a narrow extension south to Lake Tiberias, and a third sector starting about halfway along the east shore of the Lake and extending to the River Yarmuk. These had their origin in the time when Syrian troops which had taken part in the 1948 fighting were being withdrawn from Palestine back across the international frontier. It was thought desirable to keep the Israeli and Syrian forces at a distance from each other, and the idea was that in the demilitarized zone life should go on as before, with both Jews and Arabs cultivating their lands under the supervision of the chairman of the MAC, who was to be assisted by locally recruited Jewish and Arab police.

But as early as 1950 most of the business that came ISMAC's way concerned the demilitarized zone. The situation deteriorated as the Israelis gradually took control over that part of the demilitarized zone which lay inside the former international boundaries of Palestine. Israeli intentions in this respect had been apparent during the armistice negotiations, but neither Henri Vigier, who conducted the negotiations on behalf of Bunche, nor the Syrians agreed with the interpretations put on the agreement by Israel.

It was at a meeting of ISMAC in March, 1951, that Israel
first put forward its claim to full sovereignty in the demilitarized zone* in connection with a Syrian complaint that Israel
had carried out certain work there. After this Israel refused to
take part in any meetings of ISMAC if complaints concerning
the demilitarized zone were on the agenda. But in the period
for which statistics are available it appears that about 90 per
cent of the Syrian and 70 per cent of the Israeli complaints were
connected with events in the zone.

In the central sector there were a number of Arab villages
including Baggara, Ghanname and Khouri Farm. In 1951 the
inhabitants of these villages were forcibly evicted westwards
and the buildings demolished. As a result of a Security Council
resolution in May of that year the inhabitants were given permission to return home, but, according to General Burns's
book *Between Arab and Israeli*, by 1954 only 350 out of the
original 2,000 evicted had done so. The conditions under
which they then found themselves living were so bad that they
would have liked to cross over into Syria, but the Syrian
authorities prevented them from doing this. In the 1956 war
they were compelled by the Israelis to go into Syria, and are
still there, while their lands are cultivated by Israeli farmers.

A number of Arab villages in the southern sector have
suffered a similar fate. I imagine that a number of those
evicted settled somewhere in the Golan Heights and that their
children have watched the land that had been in their families
for hundreds of years being cultivated by Israeli farmers.
From time to time they opened fire on these farmers. That, of
course, was a violation of the armistice agreement, though I
could not help thinking that in similar circumstances Norwegian peasants would almost certainly have acted in the same
way.

In course of time all the Arab villages disappeared. In the
southern sector the Arabs were forcibly prevented from doing
any cultivation; in the central sector a certain amount of culti-

* The Armistice agreement between Israel and Syria was signed on
  20 July, 1949. On 19 July the Israeli Government sent identical
  telegrams to all its representatives abroad stating that the demilitarized zone was to be regarded as being under the full sovereignty
  of Israel. See Bar-Yaacov, *The Israel–Syrian Armistice*, p. 64.

vation continued, but questions of ownership were extremely complicated and led to a series of complaints and violations of the armistice; in the northern sector Israelis and Arabs continued to cultivate side by side without any particular difficulty.

Here, too, demarcation lines were not marked on the ground, which led to more trouble. Israel was firmly opposed to any idea of marking the western boundary of the demilitarized zone on the excuse that the whole of it belonged to Israel. Syria on the other hand demanded that the entire zone should be marked on the ground. As the Israelis had taken effective control over the whole area there was no chance of an agreed solution. It is pointless to argue whether Israel had or had not a legal right to do what she did. But what is certain is that her attitude made any steps towards peace impossible.

During the summer of 1963 there was more trouble in the demilitarized zone. UNTSO had tried without success to find the cultivable areas belonging to Israelis and Arabs. There had been no proper meetings of ISMAC since 1951, so that there was no opportunity for bringing the two sides together. Whenever there was a complaint the chairman of ISMAC had to negotiate with each side separately.

Levi Eshkol had succeeded Ben-Gurion as Prime Minister in June, 1963, and he was anxious to get the eastern boundaries of Israeli cultivation in the southern sector of the demilitarized zone defined. I think there were probably two reasons for this. He wanted to put a stop to the continual shooting, and he wanted to prevent the over-enthusiastic Israeli farmers from penetrating the Arab cultivable area. After a meeting with Eshkol in August I took the matter up with the Syrians, but it was over a year before I got any reply, and in the meantime Israel had tried to persuade UNTSO to agree to a line being drawn on the map which should represent the eastern limit for Israeli cultivation. It was impossible for UNTSO to say yes or no to this proposal. All we could say was that to the best of our knowledge the line shown on the map did represent the limit of cultivation, but this could only be effective if it was agreed by both the parties which had signed the original General Armistice Agreement. The Israelis used all the weapons in their armoury—charm, arguments, and more direct pressure—to win us over, but it was not possible for us to go beyond the terms of the agreement. When eventually the Syrian answer came it was along the lines that might have been expected. They were prepared to accept an eastern limit for Israeli cultivation but only provided they were able to cultivate Arab lands lying to the east of that limit. This the Israelis were not prepared to accept, so there the matter rested.

Fishing and cultivation rights were not the only occasions for trouble in the demilitarized zone, though it was these that most often led to military exchanges. On 19 August we received information that two boys from Almagor, a kibbutz north of Lake Tiberias, had been killed the previous evening. They had been victims of a military or para-military band of eight to ten men, presumably coming from Syria, though we had never had any positive evidence of this. Our observers tried to follow the tracks of the band, but unfortunately they were unable to go through the demilitarized zone to the Syrian frontier and were obliged to stop at its western limit because the Israelis had previously insisted that ISMAC personnel should ask permission before entering the zone, and the UN had mistakenly given in on this.

The day after the Almagor incident there was an exchange of fire a little further north, which was heard by two of our observation posts, Bravo and Charlie. The Syrians alleged that the Israelis had started the shooting, which had gone on for some hours, but the timing of the outbreak was not clear. Observers in OP Bravo put the first shots at 1010 without being able to say who fired them, while OP Charlie put them at 1013 and blamed the Syrians. It was reasonable to suppose that the two posts were recording the same incident, but that their watches had not been properly synchronized. This was an unfortunate error. At that period we sent out a time signal only once a day, but subsequently increased their number. As things were we were in no position to say who had fired first. When we were preparing our report on this incident we had some exchanges with Dr Bunche in New York. He sensibly remarked: 'It is doubtful whether, in a sensitive matter like this, the Secretary-General ought to present the Security Council with a mere statement of opinion. If there is evidence, conclusions can be drawn from it, but a mere expression of opinion could lead to disastrous consequences in a Security Council debate.'

So the report had to be written with extreme care. Of course, had ISMAC been functioning as it had been intended to function, it would have been the forum for discussion of the report and for a vote on it. As it was, the report had to be sent via the Secretary-General to the Security Council for a decision. Matters were not simplified by a talk I had with the Syrian Prime Minister in which he said definitely that no Syrian military had been involved. He may well have been right, since it is quite possible that the assailants belonged to a para-military group of Palestinians.

When the Security Council met it had before it an Israeli complaint over the Almagor incident and a Syrian complaint about the following day's shooting. Eventually a resolution was put forward but vetoed by the Soviet Union.

In the course of the debate the Moroccan delegate made a suggestion that the Secretary-General should prepare a report on the working of the armistice agreements between 1949 and 1963. This was agreed, and UNTSO was asked to carry out the task. I discussed it with my senior officials and gave an esti-mate that the report could be ready in two months. This proved much too optimistic. The report was not, in fact, ready till August, 1964. It had been edited by my political adviser, Henri Vigier, and was an excellent piece of work, though it proved impossible to give an analysis of all the complaints that had been made since they numbered between 30,000 and 40,000. The Secretary-General decided that, as it was neces-sarily a selective rather than a comprehensive study, it was not a suitable starting-point for a Security Council debate, and so it was never published.

Some of the conclusions reached in the report, however, are worth giving. The survey, Henri Vigier wrote, 'would not be complete without a reference to two arguments frequently used by Israeli representatives to explain why they cannot comply with a resolution of the Mixed Armistice Commission (MAC) or with requests or recommendations of the United

Nations Truce Supervision Organization (UNTSO). The first argument refers to Israel's security; the second, which is connected to the first, refers to the indivisability of the Armistice agreements ... A Party, which invokes its security for not applying provisions of the armistice agreements, should, it seems, expect that the other Party will also invoke its security for not applying the same or other provisions of the armistice agreements ... So long as for security reasons the status of the demilitarized zone and that of the defensive areas are not observed, tension will continue and occasional incidents may occur. The observance of the military clauses of the armistice agreements relating to the demilitarized zone and defensive areas would probably give Israeli and Arab farmers more security than the presence in these areas of prohibited forces and weapons.'

As a step towards reducing tension locally, following the Security Council debate, I proposed to both sides that we should carry out an inspection of the demilitarized zone and the so-called 'defensive areas' on both sides of the demarcation line to discover whether troops or weapons in excess of those permitted by the armistice agreements had been introduced. The inspection was duly carried out, but nothing new was found, though it resulted in another observer being declared *persona non grata*. He was an American Marine Corps Captain and his offence was to have requested the Syrians to remove a canvas cover over two parked armoured cars. Their presence was a clear breach of the armistice agreement, but the inhabitants of the nearby village claimed that they were part of their local defence system, and presumably reported what had happened to Damascus. The Secretary-General took the matter up with the Syrian Prime Minister but with no success. The Captain had to be transferred.

We often used inspections as a way of taking the heat out of a tense situation. Usually the parties concerned raised no objection to them, and we seldom unearthed anything of much significance because the authorities had time to remove anything they did not want to be seen. In my opinion we should have been able to carry out inspections in the demilitarized zone and defensive areas without warning.

The mistrust prevailing between Israel and Syria, which was aggravated by Syria's realization that the status quo was all the time being altered by Israel in her favour, was reflected in the most trifling matters. The Banat Yacub Bridge, where the exchange of prisoners had taken place, was one such example. The bridge lay in the demilitarized zone and until the 1967 war the only people to use it were UN personnel. It needed maintaining, but the question was who should provide it. Each side offered its services and refused to allow the honour to go to the other. For us the outcome of the comedy was important because nearly all our supplies for Damascus came from Jerusalem over the bridge and if it was out of action they would have to make a long detour through Jordan or Lebanon. Fortunately the bridge held up till 1967.

The demarcation line between Israel and Syria was about 80km long. UNTSO had ten observation posts along it, four on the Israeli side and six on the Syrian side. Additional temporary posts were set up as required.

❖   ❖   ❖

The total length of the demarcation line between Egypt and Israel was 265km—206 between Israel and Egypt proper, and 59km between Israel and Gaza. Article 8 of the armistice agreement (see Appendix II) laid down that the area round the village of El Auja was to be demilitarized and that both Egyptian and Israeli forces should be excluded from it. El Auja was on a cross-roads of great strategic importance which lent itself admirably as the starting point for an attack by Egypt against Israel or by Israel against Egypt. Israel, in fact, used El Auja for this very purpose in 1948, 1956 and 1967. The chairman of EIMAC (Egypt-Israel MAC) and the UN observers were responsible for ensuring that the demilitarization clause was adhered to but had no means of enforcing it.

The original inhabitants of the area, about 3,500 Bedouin belonging to the Azazme tribe, were driven out by Israel in 1950. Egypt complained, first to EIMAC and then to the Security Council, but without any result, even though Israel was instructed to let the tribesmen go back. In September, 1953, a kibbutz called Ketsiot was established in the area. Egypt argued that this was a purely military act since there was very little prospect of any cultivation in the area. At a meeting in September, 1954, EIMAC decided that the kibbutz was in fact organized as a unit of the Israeli army and that its presence was a violation of the armistice agreement. It should therefore be removed. But this was never done. Later the kibbutz was reinforced with police, and after a clash along the demarcation line two companies of Israeli troops occupied buildings in the area, including some which had been used as headquarters for EIMAC. Egyptians belonging to the MAC were taken prisoner, but later released.

General Burns, who was UNTSO's Chief of Staff at the time, protested to the Israeli Foreign Ministry. He was told that Israeli forces would only withdraw if the Egyptians removed posts which they were alleged to have established in the demilitarized zone and if Egyptian forces were also withdrawn from defensive positions they were occupying between the line El-Quseima–Abu Aweigila and the demilitarized zone. No action was in fact taken, and from that point onwards Israel exercised complete control over this vital strategic area. EIMAC's meetings had to be held outside the area, in Gaza.

When the Suez War started on 29 October, 1956, the Israelis declared that in their view EIMAC had ceased to exist and they took no further part in its meetings. No other Government supported this attitude, but when one party absents itself from such meetings there is no way of forcing them to come back.

After UNEF had been set up at the end of 1956 it took over most of EIMAC's functions, though EIMAC continued to function from Gaza. There were no special problems along the demarcation lines between 1956 and 1967 except for frequent overflights, mainly by Israeli planes. One such overflight, on 23 July, 1963, the anniversary of the 1952 revolution, which is celebrated as National Day in Egypt, resulted in the censure of Israel by EIMAC, a report being sent to the Security Council with the intention of reminding world opinion of what was going on.

On another occasion EIMAC, even in its crippled condition, was able to make a small positive contribution. Egypt complained that an Israeli observation post had been set up across

the demarcation line in Egyptian territory. We employed the
services of a surveyor who found that the post was just inside
Israeli territory—apparently the Egyptians were using different
maps to those which were the basis of the armistice agreements, and had a 10 metre margin of error.

※   ※   ※

Jordan's demarcation line with Israel was longer than that
of any other Arab country, extending over 570km. From the
Dead Sea down to the Gulf of Aqaba it followed the old international boundary between Palestine and Transjordan, though
this had never been marked on the ground. Apparently the
definition of the border in some areas was that it should follow the lowest point of the *wadis* (water courses) or valleys,
but this is liable to change after heavy rain—a fact which was
to cause difficulty. North of the Dead Sea there were three
places where the demarcation line widened out into a strip of
no-man's-land—the Jerusalem area, the Jebel el-Mukhabbir or
Government House area, and the Latrun area.

In the Jerusalem area the demarcation lines, which are the
same as those laid down in the cease-fire agreement of 30
November, 1948, were about 5km long and varied in breadth
from a few metres to about 600 metres. In this strip no activity
was supposed to take place without prior agreement between
the parties concerned. But the demarcation lines had been
drawn on the map with a thick wax pencil, and this line itself
represented anything from 6–40 metres on the ground. There
were a number of inhabited houses in this no-man's-land and
in 1951 a special agreement was reached whereby they could
continue to be used and the respective authorities were to go
on providing them with services—water, electricity, and so on.
In addition there were a number of military positions in the
strip, and these were maintained on the principle of preserving
the status quo. The armistice lines had in fact been drawn on
the map in 1948 in a great hurry, without any consideration for
where the military positions lay.

Over the years both sides had been creeping into the area
'between the lines', taking over unoccupied houses and setting
up military posts. This had led to a number of violations of the

armistice agreement with the consequential round of shootings, killings, woundings, complaints, investigations and meetings of the Hashemite Kingdom of Jordan–Israel Mixed Armistice Committee (HJK–IMAC), and condemnation of the guilty. A sort of competition developed to see which side could get most condemnations of the other through the MAC. This did nobody any good and simply increased the tension.

The real source of trouble was the thickness of the line drawn on the map. What did the expression 'between the lines' mean? The views held by Israel and Jordan were completely opposed to each other. Israel wanted the area between the lines to be as small as possible, that is to say for it to be calculated from the inside of the lines on the map. Jordan wanted the area to be as big as possible—to be calculated from the outside of the lines. It was impossible for us to force a ruling on the two sides, though UNTSO's natural preference was for the space separating the former combatants to be as big as it could be. This was particularly desirable in the Jerusalem area where, when sometimes only a few feet divided Arabs and Jews, armistice violations could easily begin by an exchange of abuse, followed by stone-throwing and finally by shots.

This was one of the problems discussed at a meeting of the MAC on 3 and 7 February, 1955, after two Israeli soldiers on patrol had been wounded in the Street of the Prophets in the Musrara Quarter of Jerusalem, at a spot which lay exactly under one of the thick crayon lines. According to the complaint lodged by the Jordanians the two soldiers had been challenged but had not responded; so shots had been fired. Naturally enough Israel also lodged a complaint, maintaining that the patrol had all the time been inside Israeli territory. In the course of the discussions in the MAC the Israelis insisted that there must be a ruling as to where the border lay—was it on the outside or the inside of the pencil line on the map, or did it run through the middle? The Jordanians wanted the present incident to be dealt with first and thereafter agree to what they called a 'more intelligent' definition of the line. They tabled a resolution stating that the patrol had crossed the demarcation line. The Israeli delegation immediately countered this with a point of order to the effect that 'the armistice commission confirmed that the inner edge of the line (i.e. that which made the area smallest) shall in the Jerusalem area be accepted as the limit of the demarcation line, and that this conforms to the earlier practice of the commission'. Points of order were supposed to be dealt with at once and to have priority over other resolutions. Jordan protested on the ground that the point of order contained matters of substance and because there had, contrary to what Israel implied, never been any accepted definition of the demarcation line. After a good deal of debate the Chairman allowed Israel's point of order to be taken up. It was voted on, and passed, in that Israel voted in favour while the Chairman and the Jordan delegates abstained.

The Chairman ought never to have allowed the vote on a point of order which included a matter of substance. Equally the Jordanian delegate ought to have voted against it. On this occasion the Chairman had no legal adviser sitting with him. In my time I always insisted that my legal adviser should attend these MAC meetings, since legal problems often came up in them.

This decision was to have consequences later, though it was to be ten years before Israel made capital out of it. In the meantime Israeli patrols continued to follow routes which came under the thick pencil lines, which contributed to the number of shootings and to the tension in the Jerusalem area.

In the area around Jebel el-Mukhabbir and Government House agreement had been reached that an Arab village and a Jewish agricultural school should be allowed to continue to function, but that any other activities would require special agreement. Israel proposed that the area should be divided equally between the parties, but Jordan was unable to accept this, presumably because most of the land in question was Arab and because it would mean agreeing to an enlargement of Israeli territory. So after a while both sides began creeping into this area also, the Jordanians building more houses in the Arab village as the population there increased and the Israelis building a large new hotel called the Garden of Judaea on old foundations. From time to time military positions were constructed, in spite of unavailing protests. If one side did something the other side always copied it, often adopting this course of action in preference to lodging a complaint with the MAC. Israel proved itself particularly clever at this tit-for-tat game.

Several times over the years the Security Council debated the problems of this area and passed resolutions upholding the status quo. But not only were the demarcation lines not marked on the ground but also the road between Jerusalem and Bethlehem crossed the lines in two places. Along this road went both Jordanian civil and—contrary to the armistice agreement—military traffic.

In the Latrun region there was a large area of no-man's-land, about 40–45,000 dunums* of good agricultural land. But apart from some land belonging to the Trappist Monastery which lay on the Jordanian side none of it could be cultivated without prior agreement between the parties. Even the monastery had to have its permit to cultivate renewed from month to month. In spite of this both Israelis and Jordanians did farm in the area, and eventually 5,000 dunums were under cultivation. Both sides sowed, protesting against the other doing so, but the MAC managed to arrange for the harvesting. Jordan later suggested that they and the Israelis should withdraw from the area but had difficulty in persuading their own villagers to do so. Nor were the Israelis willing to withdraw. A number of proposals for marking the demarcation lines on the ground were put forward but nothing came of them, and at intervals each side accused the other of military activity in the area.

After the 1967 war the inhabitants of several villages in the area, including among others those of Beit Nuba and Yalu, were forcibly removed and their homes destroyed. There was no question here of people being compelled to move as a result of military action. That same autumn I drove past the places where the villages had been and once or twice I noticed Arab peasants sitting around, apparently with nothing to do, in the afternoon sunlight. Once I stopped and asked one of them where the village of Yalu was. He said, 'Yalu is des-

* 1 dunum = 1000m².

60

troyed; you can only find it in our hearts.' He and others like him had not learned to forget their home, and continued to return to a spot which helped them to remember happier days.

In general it can be said that the hastily drawn-up demarcation lines between Israel and Jordan did more to encourage infiltration across the border than to check it, especially in those parts of the lines north of Jerusalem. The main reason for this was that the boundary was so drawn that the Arabs in that area were the victims of great economic hardship, since their villages were cut off from the land which for generations had been the source of their livelihood. The Jordanian villages lay on the western slopes of the Judaean hills with the fertile agricultural plain of Palestine lying spread below them to the west. Jordanian forces occupied positions on the hills inside the West Bank looking out westwards, while the Israelis held positions in the plains. The demarcation line ran roughly halfway between the two opposing military forces. The unfortunate villagers were not only cut off from the land on which they relied for a livelihood, but failed to qualify as refugees, since the UN definition of a refugee is someone who has lost his home as well as his land. This meant that many Arabs in the West Bank villages found themselves in a worse economic position than the refugees who received UN grants. It is not difficult to picture the state of desperation to which they were driven when they were obliged to contemplate Israeli farmers exploiting the land which they and their forefathers had cultivated for so many hundreds of years.

It was these sort of people who were responsible for infiltration over the demarcation line, their aim being to steal from what had not so long ago been their own land, to carry out acts of sabotage, and so on. Israel's reaction to these attacks by degrees switched towards a policy of 'massive retaliation', and so it was that a cycle was set up which it proved impossible to break. Israel always held the Jordanian Government responsible for attacks across the border, but I think that it is not unreasonable to believe General Glubb, who was for many years Commander of the Arab Legion, when he says that the Jordanian authorities did all they possibly could to stop infiltration. It was not really until 1965, nine years after

General Glubb had been dismissed from his post, that infiltration and acts of sabotage in the area became organized.

Observations of the Israel–Jordan demarcation line was conducted via stations at Jenin, Tulkarm, Latrun, Hebron, Jericho and Irbid, and these were combined with patrols along the demarcation line on the Jordanian side. The posts at Jericho and Irbid were later closed at the request of the Jordanian authorities. Temporary observation posts were in addition set up as and when needed.

*　　*　　*

The demarcation line between Israel and Lebanon presented a very different picture to that between Israel and Jordan. It was only about 80km long and followed the former international boundary. At an early stage it was agreed to mark the line on the ground, except for about 6km where the two sides maintained different interpretations of the Franco–British frontier agreement of 1923. Supervision of the agreements was carried out by patrols based at Naqura in Lebanon.

When the four armistice agreements were signed the general expectation was that they would be followed up by a proper peace settlement in a fairly short time, perhaps after a year or 18 months. When this hope proved illusory the agreements were gradually eroded. UNTSO did its best, by keeping in constant touch with all parties concerned, to get them to keep the agreements. But our experience inevitably makes for scepticism about the chances, in the Middle East setting, of a limited agreement becoming the forerunner of peace.

CHAPTER 4

JERUSALEM

✿ ✿ ✿ ✿

By an agreement signed on 7 July, 1948, the UN assumed responsibility for security in the demilitarized Mount Scopus area, which was entirely surrounded by territory held by Jordan. This area lies about 1km north-east of the Old City and extends over about 2km, including the highest point inside the Jerusalem Municipal Region. Its military significance is obvious. Whoever controls Mount Scopus controls the road northwards to Ramallah and Nablus, and eastwards towards Jericho and Amman. If Israel managed to get control of Mount Scopus it would mean that Jerusalem was more or less encircled.

The 1948 agreement covered two Jewish institutions, the Hadassah Hospital and the Hebrew University, and one Arab institution, the Augusta Victoria Hospital, the building which commemorated the visit of Emperor William II to Palestine in 1898 and was named after his Empress. It was laid down that in the Jewish area there should not be more than 85 civilian police or more than 33 civilian personnel, and in the Arab area the civilian police should not exceed 40. In addition the Mount Scopus region included the Arab village of Issawiya and a strip of no-man's-land between the Augusta Victoria Hospital and the Hebrew University.

Most of the problems in the Mount Scopus region arose from disputes over maps. The Israelis claimed that the correct map was one referred to in the original agreement, which was dated 7 July and initialled F.M.B. (Franklin M. Begley, a member of the UN Secretariat who assisted in preparation of the agreement but who did not actually sign it). The

Jordanians, on the other hand, took their stand on a map dated 21 July, 1948, when the Jordanian and Israeli Military Commanders made an agreement over the control of the strip of no-man's-land. That map was initialled by the Arab Military Commander and by Begley, but not by the Israeli Commander, and Israel had always refused to recognize it.

The 7 July map covered a larger area than the 21 July map, which meant that there was an area on Mount Scopus which the Israelis claimed was inside the demilitarized zone but which the Jordanians claimed was inside Jordan, and it was in this area that most violations of the armistice took place. Because of the different interpretations held by the two sides there was no demarcation of lines on the ground and it seemed incomprehensible to me that the head of UNTSO had not at the outset insisted on one valid map. This was all the harder to understand since UN's own representative, Franklin Begley, had initialled both maps. The UN has therefore to accept its share of responsibility for the subsequent trouble. The only explanation that can be offered is that during the period when General Riley was head of UNTSO, from September, 1948, till 1953, few if any problems arose in the Scopus region.

After 1953 Israeli Police began intensified patrol activity in the area between the 7 July and 21 July lines, aimed at proving their contention that the earlier map was the correct one.* This led to complaints by the Jordanians and shooting incidents. Israel maintained that patrols were essential for security, and gradually extended their range to Solomon's Gardens (Gan Schlomit) in the Ras el-Sullam area which was outside the perimeter fence surrounding the Hadassah Hospital and the Hebrew University. It was there that the exchange of fire took place in the course of which a Canadian observer, Colonel Flint, was killed while attempting to end the firing and rescue some Israeli policemen.

The Israelis patrolled right up to the edge of Issawiya village and seemed bent on provoking and intimidating the villagers, who found that the land open to cultivation by them

* From General Burns's book *Between Arab and Israeli* it appears that he had no special problems over the two maps, since he only mentions the 21 July one.

The Author, Jerusalem, 1970.

2   Camp 'Little Norway', Toronto, Canada. Crown Princess Märtha and Prince Hara.
    visiting the Royal Norwegian Air Force in 1940.

3   Beirut, June 1958. Left to Right: Galo Plaza, Dag Hammarskjöld, Rajishwar Da
    Indian Ambassador to Yugoslavia, the Author.

was restricted, since they were now unable to cultivate near the Hospital and University. Later the road between the village and Jerusalem was closed at night. When the road needed repairing nobody could agree who should do the work, so the villagers did it themselves. The Israeli Police promptly destroyed the villagers' work on the grounds of 'security'. This understandably increased the feeling of bitterness among the villagers and other Arabs who owned small plots in the area, and this in its turn led to shooting. It can safely be said that the actions taken by Israel in the name of security only had the effect of stimulating insecurity.

Over the years the Secretary-General himself became directly involved in the problem of Mount Scopus and sent his personal representative to Jerusalem and Amman in an effort to get the agreement of 7 July, 1948, implemented. Israel's point of view was that the Mount Scopus agreement had to be seen in connection with the Israel–Jordan armistice agreement, Article 8 of which refers to 'resumption of the normal functioning of the cultural and humanitarian institutions on Mount Scopus and free access thereto'. Jordan argued that implementation of the 7 July agreement was not bound up with the general armistice agreement and referred to a statement issued on 4 December, 1957, whereby both parties expressed their willingness to implement the Mount Scopus agreement.

It is certainly most regrettable that the activities of the cultural and humanitarian institutions on Mount Scopus were not resumed. The same could be said of other areas—the Wailing Wall in the Old City of Jerusalem, for example. But in the political conditions prevailing between 1948 and 1967 this would simply not have been possible. UNTSO had quite enough to do ensuring the safe passage of the fortnightly convoy which went to and from Mount Scopus to relieve fifty per cent of the 'garrison' and bring in supplies. Arrangements for this convoy, which went in the first and third week of each month, had been drawn up by General Riley in October, 1950. They included rules governing the rotation of personnel, the transport of baggage, food, fuel, and so on. Properly accredited visitors were allowed to join the convoy, which came under the protection of the Jordanian authorities while it passed through Jordanian territory. Before the convoy set out it was checked by UN observers in the presence of Israeli and Jordanian officials. Weapons, ammunition and military equipment of every description were forbidden, as were mail, maps or plans which might convey military information.

It was the responsibility of UNTSO to ensure that such items were not included in the convoy, but UNTSO was only able to check the baggage and not the Israeli vehicles in which it was carried. Later it was discovered that some of these contained secret compartments. At some stage UN officials were no longer allowed to be present when the baggage was unloaded at its destination. What apparently happened was that the Israeli Police in Mount Scopus started asking the UN observers who had accompanied the convoy in for coffee, so that on one or two occasions they missed the unloading. This was made a precedent and the Israelis thereafter said that the UN must stay out. UNTSO must take the blame for this dereliction of duty, and for weakly allowing the Israelis to exploit it. This of course they did to the full, and after the June War they held an exhibition to show how the UN had been hoodwinked. They put on show some of the equipment which had been smuggled up to Mount Scopus, including among other things the material for two jeeps mounted with recoilless 105mm cannons.

The worst aspect of the whole business was not so much that the Israeli Police tricked UNTSO as that UNTSO broke faith with the Jordanian authorities, who relied on the UN officials carrying out their duties according to the agreements. Whenever a similar situation arises in the future it is absolutely essential that all goods must be carried on vehicles or vessels belonging to the UN, and that UN officials must thoroughly check every stage of both the loading and the unloading processes.

Gradually the UN agreements concerning Mount Scopus were still further eroded. It became, for example, impossible either for me or for my representatives to gain access to the area between the lines of the two maps without obtaining prior permission from the Israeli Police—and this in spite of the fact that, according to the agreements, I was the person responsible for security in the demilitarized area. On several occasions we were stopped by the Israeli Police.

A short time after I had taken over I discussed the problem with my political adviser, Henri Vigier. He shook his head and smiled: 'The best you can do,' he said, 'is try to maintain the status quo as you found it when you came there.' But one thing there can be no doubt about is that the status quo had changed in many respect over the years, and always in Israel's favour. The original agreement had provided for a no-man's land of, say, 200 yards along the road between Augusta Victoria and the Hebrew University, with UN checkposts at each end. Other checkposts should have been established on the perimeter of the zone. If this had been done there would have been none of the problems caused by the two maps, and the Chief of Staff of UNTSO would have been able to maintain his control over the demilitarized area effectively.

* * *

Early in the morning of 25 August, 1963, I was woken by the duty officer, Major Yancy, who, after being declared *persona non grata* in Syria, was now on Headquarters staff in Jerusalem. He reported considerable firing between Israeli and Jordanian forces inside the City, so I went out on to the balcony to watch. The chairman of the HJK–IMAC managed to get both sides together for a meeting at 0500, at which the time for a ceasefire was agreed as well as for a subsequent investigation.

This was just one of many similar incidents at that time. As so often it turned out to have started more or less accidentally. As has been mentioned, the demarcation lines in the Jerusalem area were in places only a few yards apart. Troops on either side would start shouting insults at each other which would lead to stone-throwing and eventually to shooting. That is what had happened on this occasion.

However, as the shooting went on for several hours, this was a more serious incident than most. The next day I was invited to visit the monastery of St Saviour, which lay close to the demarcation lines on the Jordanian side. It was used as a school for about 130 orphans and I was taken to see one of their dormitories, which bore the marks of the previous night's exchanges. Fortunately the children had been moved to a cellar for safety and escaped injury. A little later I was called to the Israeli Foreign Office for a meeting with the Foreign Minister, Golda Meir, to discuss the incident. She said she thought it was a purely local incident and should be treated as such, adding that though it was difficult to say who started it she would emphasize that the Israelis only shot at military targets. I said I had just come from the monastery of St Saviour where I had seen several bullet holes in the children's dormitory. At that even Golda Meir was for once silent.

An incident such as this should normally have been dealt with at a meeting of HJK–IMAC and disposed of by a statement from the chairman. Both sides were agreed about this, but Israel wanted to put the matter off until after the Security Council had debated the Almagor affair (see p. 52). This annoyed the Jordanians, and the result was that each side submitted a resolution condemning the other. As on so many other occasions before and after, the chairman's vote proved decisive and both parties were censured.

After the exchange of prisoners between Syria and Israel already mentioned, which took place in December, my family celebrated Christmas peacefully in Jerusalem. Then we went to Aqaba and paid a visit to the extraordinary Wadi Rum, where some of the scenes for the film *Lawrence of Arabia* were shot. It was very cold, and huge icicles hung from the hills.

But our holiday was not to be of long duration. We received notification that Pope Paul VI's pilgrimage to the Holy Land was to take place from 4 to 6 January and the UN was asked for its co-operation. Naturally all arrangements were primarily the responsibility of the Israeli and Jordanian authorities, but they both wanted UNTSO to have a share in carrying them out. The Pope was to come first to the Old City, entering through the Damascus Gate which was only a few yards from the demarcation line, which he was subsequently to cross twice, first on his way to Nazareth on 5 January and then again on his way back to Jerusalem. The Secretary-General was a bit worried about this programme and made it clear that the UN could not itself take any responsibility for seeing it implemented. We would be there, as observers, and we would hope that our presence would help to calm things down.

Two days before the Pope was due to arrive we had discussions with the Israeli and Jordanian authorities and it was agreed that we should station observers at the point on the Jenin–Megiddo road where the Pope was to cross the demarcation line going north, and at the other crossing point, which was to be the Mandelbaum Gate in Jerusalem. We were also to have observers on Mount Zion, on the Israeli side, and at Abu Tor, which lies a little way from it.

The Pope's first stop was in Amman, but his arrival in Jerusalem was delayed because he stopped on the way at several places he wanted to see, including the traditional site on the River Jordan where Christ is supposed to have been baptized. It was a bitterly cold day, and those of us who were waiting outside the Damascus Gate stood and froze. I particularly recall my good friend Stig Mauritz Möllersward, once a UN observer and now Swedish Consul-General in Jerusalem, standing for hours in morning dress without an overcoat. Not surprisingly he caught a severe cold.

There were a number of Italian pilgrims waiting by the Damascus Gate who, by their tumultuous reception of their fellow countrymen, caused total chaos at the moment when the Pope actually arrived. It was only with great difficulty that he could be got inside the Gate, which was then shut. The rest of us failed to get through, so we missed seeing the Pope's visit to the Holy Sepulchre. But at ten in the evening my wife and I were present at St Anne's, a Greek Catholic Church dating from crusading times and one of the most beautiful in Jerusalem. Here the Pope spoke briefly before going to the Garden of Gethsemane to pray.

The next day was the day for the Pope's visit to Nazareth, where he received a joyful welcome from the largely Christian population. I had gone there early but returned to Jerusalem ahead of the Pope, who went on to Capernaum, to supervise arrangements for his passing through the Mandelbaum Gate. All went well, and on the final day of the visit Henri Vigier and I were received in audience by the Pope who thanked us for the part which we had played in the arrangements.

In the late spring of 1964 rumours began to circulate that Israel was proposing to celebrate its Independence Day, 15 May, with a parade in Jerusalem. Jordan lodged a protest, claiming that this would be a violation of the armistice agreement. Israel this time recognized the validity of the objection and the parade was held in the desert area at Beersheba. I attended this impressive occasion. There were about 200 planes in the flypast, including some eighty per cent of the Air Force Mirages. According to Press reports Israel was then spending $271m (about thirty-one per cent of its budget) on arms, Egypt $290m, and Syria $91m. These figures were to rise steeply in the coming years, and by the time of the 1967 war some Middle East countries were devoting nearly two-thirds of their budget to arms.

When I came back to Jerusalem on 14 May a huge Star of David and the figure 16 (it was the sixteenth anniversary of the State's founding) were blazing on Mount Scopus. This was a clear infringement of the armistice agreement, but although protests were lodged by both UNTSO and Jordan it was repeated year after year.

In February, 1965, I was asked to intervene in a case which was very much outside the usual run of UN business. Professor Beller of the Hadassah Hospital came to see me about what he called a 'human problem'—the arrest in Damascus of Elie Cohn. Cohn was a Jew who had entered Syria on an Argentinian passport, posing as a patriotic Syrian national who had made good in South America and now wanted to make his home in his native land. He soon got on intimate terms with leading members of the Government and armed forces and was allowed to tour military installations on the Golan Heights. All the time Cohn was sending information back to Israel by means of a transmitter installed in his house. A book, which probably is not wholly accurate, called *Our Man in Damascus*, has been written about him. According to this he was arrested shortly after reports of a Government meeting in Damascus had been broadcast by Israeli radio only a little time after it had taken place. Radio detectors pinpointed the transmitter and Cohn was discovered in the act of sending messages over it. There was not much we could do for him, and he was sentenced to death. A powerful international movement to get him exchanged or reprieved was set on foot and two well-known French lawyers were among those who took up his cause, but he was hanged in Damascus on 18 May, 1965. After his execution the Israelis asked me to use my good offices to get his body returned to Israel, but the Syrians refused this on the grounds that he had already been buried and that exhumation was illegal. The only thing we did manage to do was to obtain three letters which Cohn had written before being executed. These were delivered to Israel via the MAC.

CHAPTER 5

TENSION MOUNTS

✾ ✾ ✾ ✾

The Twenty-eighth of May, 1964, is the date which marks the beginning of the escalation of the conflict which was to erupt in June, 1967, for it was then that Israel began pumping water from the River Jordan to irrigate the Negev. Arab reaction to this move was not long delayed. At a meeting in Alexandria on 7 September five Arab Governments resolved to counter Israel's action by drawing off water from two of the streams which feed the Jordan—the Hasbani in Lebanon and the Baniyas in Syria. The idea was to draw off the water from these two tributaries eastwards, then divert it south through Syrian and Jordanian territory to rejoin the river south of Lake Tiberias inside Jordan. The meeting also decided to set up a joint Arab command with General Hakim Amer as its Commander-in-Chief. The communiqué issued at the end of the meeting included a number of general threats against Israel, stating that it was 'the intention of the Arab nation to liberate Palestine from Zionist imperialism'. The same meeting gave the signal for the creation of the Palestine Liberation Organization (PLO) with its own Army (PLA). The recruiting and training of guerrillas began. These steps led to countermeasures by Israel, aimed at destroying the new movement and carrying out reprisals for any sabotage or terrorist activities launched by the Arabs.

The first leader of the PLO was a Palestinian called Ahmed Shukeiry, a lawyer who managed to do the cause with which he was supposed to be identified incalculable harm. He was a fanatical windbag whose bloodthirsty speeches were a godsend to the Israeli propaganda machine. Several Arab leaders

72

became quickly disillusioned with him. King Hussein, in a speech in June, 1966, said that he felt obliged to give up any hope of collaboration with the PLO under its existing leadership. This speech was aimed at Shukeiry, who retaliated by saying that the PLO had now no alternative but to work for the destruction of the existing régime in Jordan.

A small episode which I witnessed as early as the spring of 1964 illustrated the bad blood between these two men. Henri Vigier and I had been invited to attend the parade at Zerka marking the celebration of Jordan's Army Day. We and the rest of the guests were waiting for the King and the Crown Prince to arrive, and two vacant seats in front had been prepared for them. Then Shukeiry arrived and sat down in one of the two empty chairs. When the royal party came the situation had to be resolved by hurriedly producing a third chair. Shukeiry, as Vigier said to me later, was demonstrating his claim to be recognized as the first President of a Republican Jordan. But when the Six Day War came in 1967 Shukeiry, with much else, was finally swept away.

Israel in its turn reacted strongly to the Alexandria meeting. M. R. Kidron, head of the armistice affairs section of the Foreign Ministry, sent me a letter in September drawing my attention to resolutions passed at the meeting: 'I assume that you will take steps to remind the authorities in these States of their obligations under the agreements, which do not permit their engaging in activities such as those which were planned and organized at the meeting in Alexandria.' Kidron had occupied this post since shortly after my arrival in 1963. He was an extremely able official who stuck closely to his terms of reference, with a persuasive manner which one had to be on one's guard against. In private he could be most charming.

On 23 October, 1964, we were told by Damascus that the new Israeli representative on ISMAC had informed the chairman that work was to be started the next week on a patrol road in the area of Tel Dan, or Tel el-Qadi to use the Arab name which appeared on the map accompanying the armistice agreement. Tel Dan is in the far north of Israel, close to the demarcation line with Syria. 'Tel' means a man-made hill or mound and 'Dan' refers of course to one of the twelve tribes which received land in this area after the original Jewish settlement. The River Dan, one of the headwaters of the River Jordan, has its source in this area, and there is also a reservoir in the area. The Israelis asserted that all the springs which feed the River Dan rise inside Israeli territory and claimed that repairing the road and the drainage ditch which ran parallel to it would simply restore the situation that had existed in 1961–2 when, they claimed, both Syria and UNTSO had agreed that the area was inside Israel. But the Syrian authorities had never accepted this. They insisted that the road entered Syrian territory and claimed that several of the springs which fed the river and reservoir, and part of the reservoir itself, lay inside Syria.

Once again we were confronted with problems which owed their origin to the fact that lines had never been marked on the ground. The French Consul-General in Jerusalem once told the chairman of ILMAC that during the Second World War he had been serving with a French cavalry unit in the area, and had got to know the arguments between Britain and France over the reservoir. The French, he said, had always asserted that it was in Syrian territory and his unit used to water their horses there. In 1963 a Canadian survey team, headed by Captain Reichert, was sent with the agreement of both sides to make surveys for the purpose of ascertaining where the demarcation line lay, but it was stopped by the Israelis about 250 yards west of Tel el-Qadi. Israel then insisted that no further surveys were necessary because there had never been any complaints about the road east of the point where the team had been stopped. But the Syrians persisted in their claim that the road passed through their territory and in their refusal to let Israel use this section of the road.

It was obvious that only a neutral survey could sort out the rights and wrongs of this situation. Syria had not objected to the Reichert survey eighteen months earlier, which was presumably why Israel thought Syria accepted at least that part of the survey which had been completed before the team was stopped 250 yards short of the disputed area. But now the Syrians made it clear that they did not accept the Reichert survey; they said they would prefer the task to be carried out by a Swedish team. Their main objection to Reichert was that they had no knowledge of the documents which has been used by his team in their survey. Apparently my predecessor, General Von Horn, had not included these documents in the survey results when he forwarded them to the two parties. One of the documents was a survey which the British had made in 1941, in which they asserted that the whole reservoir was in Palestinian territory, but obviously a survey like this, on which only one of the two Mandatory powers involved was represented, was not of much use, and not surprisingly its conclusion was not acceptable to France, or, later, to Syria. If the work of an international team was to be of any value it would have to have access to the material which the Franco–British Border Commission of 1923 had had before it. We learned, through the UN Secretariat, that most of the material belonging to the British authorities in Palestine had passed into the hands of Israel, and most of the material on the French side had gone to Syria.

We tried to persuade the Israelis to stop work on the road until we could be sure of its true relationship to the demarcation lines. But on 2 November we received a report from OP 1, situated on Tel el-Qadi, to the effect that the Israelis were working on the patrol road, and the next day they moved their bulldozers into the disputed area. The Syrians opened fire on them from the village of Nukheila, in Syria, north of Tel el-Qadi. After eighty minutes the chairman of ISMAC managed to get the shooting stopped. Both sides lodged complaints and an investigation was started. At the same time UNTSO issued a warning to both sides; Israel was told not to send its people into the area until the position of the demarcation line had been determined, and Syria was told to stop shooting and bring its complaints before ISMAC.

Tension increased and both sides stepped up their military preparations. On 13 November Israel sent a patrol along the road in the disputed area north of Tel el-Qadi and an intensive exchange of fire followed. The chairman of ISMAC was at first unable to arrange a ceasefire because it was impossible to locate the Syrian delegation. When he had succeeded in doing this he was told by the Israelis that they had not been able to contact all their formations, and a few minutes before the ceasefire was due to start Israel sent in planes for the first time since 1951. At last, however, we did manage to get the shooting stopped.

Use of planes was an extremely serious escalation of the fighting, and resulted in much more extensive damage than that caused in the usual ground encounters. OP 1 was in the middle of the area which became a target for the Syrian artillery and a 120mm mortar shell fell on the roof of the post's shelter without exploding. This was just as well, because it was not constructed to withstand a projectile of this calibre. The observers, with the most commendable devotion to duty, continued to transmit reports throughout the firing. Casualties on the Israeli side were four killed and seven wounded. The Syrians gave their casualties as seven killed and twenty-six wounded, but the number killed was probably a good deal higher. Damage to villages on both sides was also considerable.

We instituted an immediate and thorough investigation of the incident, which took eleven days to complete. Both Israel and Syria complained to the Security Council, which received copies of our report. Since the incident had been of such a serious nature I arranged for personal meetings with the Israeli and Syrian authorities to hear their views. To Lavavi, Director-General at the Israeli Foreign Ministry, I expressed my great regret that planes had been sent in. His answer was that this was the only way in which they could stop the Syrians from firing on the kibbutzes. When I went to Damascus I met General Jedid, the Syrian Chief of Staff who was also Minister of Defence. He emphasized that this could not be regarded as a purely local incident, since there could be no doubt, in his opinion, that the disputed road passed through Syrian territory.

Israel continued to send occasional patrols along the road, but fortunately there were no more serious incidents, though there was some shooting. Both sides had accepted the idea that a Swedish expert should look at the problem, and Professor Lars Asplund was chosen for the job. The Israelis argued that Asplund ought to start work where Reichert had left off —i.e. 250 yards west of Tel el-Qadi, and that he should include the patrol road and the demarcation line beyond the disputed area and further to the east. This would bring him up against new problems, including the so-called '60 metre strip' in the demilitarized zone, where Israelis and Arabs cultivated the soil in close proximity to each other. The Syrians objected to this. What was needed now, they said, was a decision about Tel el-Qadi and the patrol road. They argued that to pursue the survey to the east would only complicate matters by introducing a whole lot of fresh material. So there was deadlock.

On 17 March fighting broke out again. An Israeli patrol vehicle on the road north of Tel el-Qadi was fired on and the Israelis returned the fire. They also directed their fire against construction work which the Arabs had started on a nearby hill in connection with the scheme for diverting the waters of the Baniyas and Hasbani Rivers. This was the first time that the diversion plan had been involved in the fighting, and now it had become mixed up with the Tel el-Qadi border issue.

Professor Asplund arrived in Jerusalem on 29 April and quickly got in touch with all the interested parties. As early as 6 May he was able to produce a first report which included his proposals for a solution of the border dispute. He then returned to Sweden.

Tension over the diversion of the Jordan waters continued to grow. On 13 May there was a report of shooting in the central sector of the demilitarized zone near the Banat Yacub Bridge. This was a purely one-sided operation, directed by the Israelis against tractors, bulldozers, and earth-moving equipment in the area, and was obviously intended to interfere with work on the Hasbani and Baniyas diversion plans. Some of our observers, who were crossing the bridge on their way from Tiberias to Damascus, reported that before the firing began the Israelis had stopped the movement of civilians in the area.

At about this time the Israeli Prime Minister, Levi Eshkol, made a speech which contained a strong warning to the Arab countries against diverting the headwaters of the Jordan. He said that any attempt to deprive Israel of the water to which, according to the Johnson Plan* she was legally entitled, would

* This Plan, put forward by the American Government's special envoy, Eric Johnson, in 1955, would have given Arab countries

be regarded as an act of aggression. Storm clouds were gathering.

Nor did we get any dividends out of Professor Asplund's efforts. Neither side made any response to his proposals and after a while the whole matter was dropped. A lot of valuable work was thrown away, even though Israel did cease its patrols along the road. The obvious lesson from this affair is that in future all demarcation lines must be marked on the ground, if the job of neutral observers is to be effective. As it was we were obliged to waste endless time and trouble on the most trivial complaints.

* * *

'Grave situation in Jerusalem. Return at once.' This message reached me on 15 August, 1965, at a sub-station in the South Lebanese village of Merjayoun. I had taken a couple of days' holiday to attend the Baalbek Festival and was now inspecting a telecommunications post which was shortly to be withdrawn, having been rendered obsolete by new radio equipment that had been issued to us. That same afternoon I was back in Jerusalem, where Colonel Marsh informed me of an ultimatum he had received from the Jordanian Foreign Minister, Hazem Nusseibeh, to the effect that if work on a house on the demarcation line was not stopped before noon it would be shelled. Marsh had succeeded in getting the deadline put off.

The senior Jordanian delegate on the HJK–IMAC insisted that the house was in no-man's-land and said that the Israelis had been working on it for several days. The first official Jordanian complaint had been lodged on 13 August. At an emergency meeting of the MAC it was agreed to investigate the Jordanian complaint.

This investigation showed that part of the house lay in Israeli territory while the rest of the building was in the 'thick line' (see page 57) which on the ground could be anything from 6 to 40 metres wide. Israel's answer to the Jordanian

sixty per cent of the combined water of the River Jordan and its tributaries, and Israel forty per cent. Largely owing to Syrian opposition the plan was never adopted. The Israelis, too, objected to the share of water they were to receive and to the concept of the plan being under international supervision.

complaint was to refer to the 1955 decision in the MAC which accepted the outer edge of the 'thick line' as the true line of demarcation. That decision, it will be recalled, had only Israel's vote in its favour, the chairman and the Jordanian representative having abstained. But if this decision was valid the whole house was inside Israel. So, after ten years, the muddled handling of one session of the MAC brought its harvest of serious trouble.

It might be supposed that our first step would have been to call a fresh meeting of the MAC, but the armistice machinery was not as simple as that. All complaints were filed as they came in, and had to be dealt with in their correct order, although some might be much more urgent than others. This could mean that days and even weeks would pass before a really serious matter came up for consideration before the commission. We had suggested to headquarters in New York that some system of priorities ought to be worked out, but our suggestion had been turned down.

Jordan's senior delegate on the MAC, Colonel Dahoud, telephoned several times during the course of that day, 15 August, to report that the Israelis were continuing to work on the house. They had opened a window which had been blocked up, and it looked as though they were planning to turn it into a military post. Marsh got in touch with the Israeli Foreign Ministry and asked them to stop work until the matter had come before the MAC. The Israelis said they would stop work for one day. This persuaded the Jordanians that the Israelis had realized the threat to shell the house was not bluff, and could have led to serious shooting and loss of life. The Jordanians also accused Israel of concentrating troops near the house, but as the MAC headquarters were only a few yards away we were able to inspect both sides and found no evidence of this.

The affair was reported to Bunche in New York with a request that the Secretary-General or his representative should contact the delegations of Israel and Jordan. I myself repeated the appeal to Israel to stop work on the house until the MAC had met and asked Jordan not to start any shooting. The Secretary-General made a similar appeal on 16 August, pointing out that, though both Israel and Jordan had previously said they wanted to keep tension at as low a level as possible, especially in Jerusalem, the steps which they had been taking tended to increase tension. Israel now agreed to postpone work on the house for a further week.

On 19 August I had a meeting with Golda Meir, the Foreign Minister, but this was unproductive as she simply repeated her Government's reliance on the 1955 resolution of the MAC. Nor did I gain the impression that work would be held up until the MAC had met. I was also in continuous touch with the Jordanian authorities on the matter.

On 20 August we were told by the Jordanians that Israeli troops were in the house and had mounted machine-guns on the roof. Investigation showed this information to be incorrect. The next day I received a request from the Jordanian Prime Minister, Wasfi Tel, for a meeting. This took place in Amman the same afternoon. He repeated the warning that they would shell the house unless the Israelis stopped work on it. I tried to calm him down by saying that the Secretary-General was personally involved in the matter, and I told him I thought that if the MAC was allowed to continue its mediation it would be able to find a solution. I also pointed out that over the past two years four military positions, two Israeli and two Jordanian, had been constructed or renovated either in the 'thick line' area or in no-man's-land. The UN had managed to get two of these removed, but two remained—the house which all the present trouble was about, and a building which the Jordanians had put up as a military post in October, 1964. This too was partly under the 'thick line' and partly in no-man's-land, but the Israelis had made no complaint about it. Wasfi Tel professed to see no resemblance between the Jordanian house and the one the Israelis were currently trying to reinforce. As far as I could make out his argument was that since the Israelis had not complained it meant they accepted the Jordanian post. But this was part of the game of tit for tat continuously played by the two sides, and on this occasion it appeared that the Israelis had a good card in their hand to play. As I left my meeting with the Prime Minister I was able to see that the King and the rest of the cabinet were waiting

Government House, Jerusalem: Headquarters of UNTSO.

The convoy to Mount Scopus. In front is an Israeli armoured vehicle which probably contained many hidden compartments.

6 *Memorial Service in the Holy Sepulchre, Jerusalem, after the death of Pope John XX.*
   Next to the Author is Lt-Colonel Stig Mauritz Möllersward.

7 *Pope Paul VI's pilgrimage to the Holy Land, 4–6 January, 1964.*

in an adjoining room to learn how our talk had gone. I knew the situation was explosive because in September another Arab summit was due and the Jordanians probably felt this was no time for them to appear to be making concessions.

It became clear to me that if we were to get anywhere in this particular problem we should have to keep out of the complex legal arguments on which both sides based their cases. If we called a meeting of HJK–IMAC we could be quite certain that the 1955 resolution would come up and that that would get us nowhere. Bunche, too, was of the opinion that we should try to avoid such a meeting, and thought the best plan might be for me, as UNTSO Chief of Staff, to take an initiative aimed at a tacit agreement for the neutralization of the two houses, which in fact were situated less than 100 yards from each other. I thought the best way of ensuring that the houses were neutralized would be for anything of a military nature to be removed from them. Bunche, who had been talking with members of the Israeli and Jordanian delegations in New York, thought it might be rather humiliating to insist on anything actually being taken away: what was important, he said, was to be sure that the houses were not used. I was particularly anxious for a peaceful solution of this problem because of the proximity of the headquarters of the MAC to the two disputed houses. If shooting started our people were liable to find themselves caught in very uncomfortable cross-fire. So I took up the question of 'demilitarizing' the two houses with both sides, though without much success. The Israelis said they wanted to be able to use their house for the protection of their patrols, should this be necessary, and claimed that it had been used for this purpose for a long time. There was nothing to stop them going into the house through the entrance which lay inside Israel; it was only if they took their weapons further into the house that they gave grounds for the Jordanians to object.

On 3 September I got a message from Bunche saying that Israel was now prepared to stop all work on the house for good, and was willing to keep everybody out of the house except when it was felt necessary to give cover to patrols from it. I contacted Kidron at the Israeli Foreign Ministry and asked him for confirmation. He said that work would only be stopped for two months, that is until I came back from a holiday which I was planning. He confirmed this temporary arrangement by letter. So we could record progress, though the problem was still not solved.

Shortly afterwards I had another meeting with Wasfi Tel. He agreed to a two months' postponement of Jordan's threat, provided the Israelis really did cease all work on the house. Unfortunately Israeli troops had been seen in the house the day before; otherwise I think he might have been willing to agree to the proposal that Israel should continue to use the house as before but without adding anything to it. So I had to approach Kidron again to persuade the Israelis to be discreet in their movements so that they would not be observed.

Kidron insisted that the patrols would have to be in the house whenever the fortnightly convoy left for Mount Scopus. We checked, and found that there were plenty of other buildings from which the Israelis could get just as good a view of the convoy's progress as they could from this one. This confirmed our opinion that it was a matter of principle that the Israelis were concerned with rather than any intrinsic value which the house might have for them.

On 11 September I had a meeting with the acting Foreign Minister of Jordan, Hatem Zu'by, who said that for Jordan to accept the solution the UN put forward it was essential that the house should be kept under continuous observation by UNTSO. The outline of a compromise was beginning to emerge. After further meetings with Kidron and Wasfi Tel, we were by 21 September able to consolidate agreement along the following lines: no work was to be done on the house for the next two months; Israel could use it twice a month for observation of the Mount Scopus convoy, but at other times the house should be empty. Israel made the reservation that in a time of crisis they would use it; otherwise the MAC should keep the house under observation. When, in fact, the two months had passed a new sort of status quo had come into being and the affair of the houses never became an issue again.

There was another rather similar controversy going on at the same time, but it never developed the same explosive proportions. It had been agreed in 1951 that, where houses in no-man's-land in the Jerusalem Sector were inhabited, people could go on living in them, each of the parties being responsible for the services (water, electricity, refuse collection, and so on) of the houses on its side of the strip. At the beginning of September the Israeli authorities gave notice that they were going to start extensive clearance work on their side of the strip, and moved in heavy machinery for the purpose. Jordan protested, but the work went ahead. If the MAC had not already been actively engaged in negotiations between the two parties on another matter this was just the sort of argument which could have escalated into something serious.

From the day when the house in no-man's-land first came to the boil to the day when the compromise agreement was reached was only five weeks, but for me it was one of the most difficult times of all my years in the Middle East. This was partly due to the constant exchanges of messages with New York which, owing to the difference of time, kept us up night after night. By the end of it all both my legal adviser, A. Leriche, and myself were seriously ill—and all, we could not help feeling, on account of an essentially petty business. Still, the consolation was that not a shot had been fired.

On 24 September I returned to Norway for the start of my leave. I had now completed two and a half years as Chief of Staff of UNTSO, and in March had agreed to renew my contract for another two years. So from Norway I went on to New York for consultations. The evening I arrived I felt ill, tired and very thirsty. I consulted the UN doctor who told me I had caught a cold. So I went ahead with my engagements, including a lunch the next day given by U Thant to which Crown Prince Harald of Norway, Bunche, and a number of Norwegian diplomats and members of the Secretariat had been invited. But now I was feeling completely miserable and this time the doctor, seeing the yellow in my eyes, diagnosed hepatitis and told me it would break out in a couple of days. He advised me to get out of New York. I took his advice and flew back to Oslo, where a bed had been reserved for me in Ulleval Hospital. Here Professor Anton Jervell looked after me splendidly for four weeks, and it was thanks largely to him that I managed to regain my health completely. As hepatitis is a rare disease in Norway I became a subject for the Professor's lectures and an object of much interest to his students.

Though I had been advised to prolong my convalescence till March I decided to fly back to Jerusalem on 16 January. It had, fortunately, been a comparatively peaceful time while I was away.

*   *   *

At the beginning of 1965 a new element began to make itself felt in the Middle East equation. There had already been some sporadic activity against Israel by Palestinian infiltrators, but now they showed themselves better organized and capable of infiltrating Israel from Lebanese and Jordanian territory. We started hearing the name of El Fateh.

In February the Israeli representative on the Israel–Lebanese MAC produced what was claimed to be reliable evidence that groups of saboteurs were operating from Lebanon. I was asked to make it clear to the Lebanese authorities that they would be held responsible by Israel for the activities of the guerrillas, and that these could lead to grave consequences. He quoted from a communiqué put out by a Palestinian organization in Beirut which boasted of acts of sabotage committed inside Israel. One of these saboteurs had, in fact, been captured by the Israelis and sentenced to fifteen years' imprisonment.

After this came a regular stream of complaints from both sides about breaches of the armistice agreement. Particularly serious were those in the air. In 1964–5 the MAC had before it no fewer than 419 complaints of overflying, of which 382 were laid against Israel. The Lebanese asserted that Israeli planes had penetrated 120km inside their country. I appealed to both sides to refrain from reconnaissance flights, which I felt could be more serious than casual encounters on the ground.

In February there were reports of explosives placed, presumably by Palestinian saboteurs, inside houses and silos in Israeli villages. Israel sent its complaints to the Secretary-General of the UN, who passed them on to the Security Council. Israel insisted that the Government of Jordan must take full responsibility for all acts committed by groups operating from its territory, whereas Jordan disclaimed responsibility.

In March I discussed the Israeli complaint with the Jordanian Foreign Minister, Dr Hazem Nusseibeh—a member of one of the oldest families in Jerusalem, which, for four hundred years, had been custodian of the keys of the Holy Sepulchre (the Christian communities being unable to agree among themselves who should hold them). He assured me that Jordan would do all it could to uphold the armistice agreement. In May there were several fresh acts of sabotage, which I discussed in Amman with the Prime Minister, Wasfi Tel. I told him again that the Israelis held Jordan responsible—a point of view he was unable to accept. The Jordanian authorities gave no support to the guerrillas' activities, but the border between Jordan and Israel was a long one and many of the villagers on the Jordanian side actively sympathized with the Palestinians.

On 25 August HJK–IMAC received yet another complaint of sabotage from the Israelis. Three men were said to have entered from Jordan and attacked Ramat Hakoresh, subsequently returning to Jordan in the neighbourhood of Qalqiliya. Two days later there was a similar incident in which two men, also alleged to have come from Jordan, placed an explosives charge in a building in Afula injuring two people. According to the Israelis, footprints showed that the saboteurs had subsequently re-entered Jordan.

Israel struck back. A military force crossed the border and blew up several houses in Qalqiliya. The same night another detachment crossed in the vicinity of Muqeibila in Israel in the direction of Jenin, using small arms and artillery. Another Israeli patrol entered Northern Jordan near Shuna, destroying several houses and killing two people.

So the pattern was set. Saboteurs enter Israel from Jordan or another Arab country, carry out their mission and then withdraw. Israel holds the country from which they operate responsible, and after a while launches a massive reprisal. Clearly the use by Israel in these reprisal raids of units from its regular forces was a violation of the armistice agreement, and Israel accordingly faced condemnation in the MACs. The case of individual saboteurs was more complex. Where the Arab Government concerned denied all responsibility the MAC could condemn the act of sabotage but found it harder to condemn the Government in view of the obvious difficulty of controlling all activities over the demarcation line. There could be no doubt that refugees who had lost property in what used to be Palestine were eager for revenge, and that from the beginning of 1965 they had been organized by Fateh Command. HJK–IMAC was going to have its hands full.

Guerrilla forces in Egypt came under Egyptian command, and in Syria under Syrian command. But the same was not true of Lebanon, which was later to have so many problems with the guerrillas, nor was it true of Jordan, where half the population consisted of Palestinian Arabs.

In May there was a fairly considerable outburst of shooting in Jerusalem. The Israelis claimed that the shots had originated from a Jordanian military post inside the Old City, and that they had been directed against targets in Israel, killing and wounding a number of people. There was a great outcry in the Israeli press and I was invited for an interview by the Foreign Minister, Golda Meir. Speaking with much vigour, she insisted that the Jordanian authorities should be told of the gravity with which Israel regarded the incident. We immediately sent a message to this effect to Amman. As this was a purely military affair the procedure for dealing with it was straightforward. A meeting of the MAC was called in which the chairman voted to censure Jordan and abstained on the resolution put forward by the Jordanian delegate.

On 17 May Levi Eshkol, the Israeli Prime Minister, made a proposal for direct negotiations aimed at converting the armistice agreements into a permanent peace. But this proposal was doomed from the start because the Arabs had always firmly rejected the idea of direct negotiations on the grounds that this would imply recognition of Israel and so throw away one of their strongest bargaining cards. The Jordanian answer to Eshkol came in a statement by a Government spokesman: 'The Palestine problem is a problem of belief and principle. It is not a problem of interests or resources.'

In the course of the spring I discussed the activities of Fateh with the new Lebanese President, Charles Helou. He would have liked to see an end to these activities but was just as pessimistic about the general Middle East situation as had been his predecessor, Fuad Chehab. I had had a talk with President Chehab shortly before his term of office expired in 1964, and found him gloomy about the future. He was a patriot, and in general extremely popular, though he had some enemies, as was to be expected for a man who tried to take a long-term view of what was best for his country.

Meanwhile the perennial problem of the demilitarized zone between Israel and Syria had reared its head again. As has already been mentioned, Israel had suggested that a line should be drawn marking the boundary of permitted Israeli cultivation. This the Syrians might be willing to accept on the assumption that they would be able to cultivate the land on the other side of the line. Thus the Syrians might be prepared to respect the line without in so many words acknowledging its existence. We continued to negotiate in this sense, and managed to persuade the Israelis to postpone their plans for ploughing in the area they laid claim to. But as negotiations got bogged down Israeli farmers went ahead and began to plough. This was predictably the signal for a fresh exchange of fire, but the Israelis managed to carry on, with the help of armoured tractors which were given military protection. Temporary observation posts established by the UN in the demilitarized zone helped to calm the atmosphere somewhat.

Similarly mobile observation posts were from time to time established in the neighbourhood of Almagor, just north of Lake Tiberias, when work was due to be undertaken there. The demarcation line in this area was not marked on the ground and there was uncertainty as to where it ran, and it was at the request of Kidron and the Israeli Foreign Ministry that we arranged for mobile posts at the time of ploughing, harvesting, and so on. This did not prevent fairly continuous shooting and, though I requested the Israelis to hold up agricultural work for the time being, the shooting went on. I discussed the matter with General Jedid, asking Syria to observe the armistice agreement while negotiations continued. But once again we came up against the old obstacle—the Syrians wanted the entire demarcation line to be marked on the ground, whereas the Israelis only wanted the areas which were in dispute to be marked and that there should be no demarcation of the western boundary of the zone. In March, 1965, there was a serious exchange of fire near Almagor in the course of which an Israeli tractor-driver was killed.

With a view to checking the escalation of violence I proposed that an inspection should be made of both the demilitarized zone and the so-called defensive areas on either side of the demarcation zone. There had been no inspection since 1963, and after some hesitation both Governments agreed to a new one. The results of such inspections are usually perfectly predictable, since permission has to be given before they can be carried out (the idea of surprise inspections having been turned down by the parties concerned). To coincide with the inspection I issued a fresh appeal to Israel and Syria to refrain from shooting in accordance with the Security Council Resolution of 15 July, 1948, and its confirmation on 11 August, 1949.

We had also continuing trouble on Mount Scopus where, as has already been recounted, Israel and Jordan each worked off a different map. This time trouble arose over the 1964 olive harvest. The Arab villagers of Issawiya wanted to be able to harvest the olives on the trees which grew on the western slopes of the hill, and after three weeks of negotiation the Israelis agreed to this, but on condition that Israeli Police from Mount Scopus, accompanied by a UN observer, supervised the harvest from a position a hundred yards off.

I was on a tour round the various MACs, aimed at wishing them all a happy Christmas, when on 23 December, on my way back to Jerusalem from Gaza, I received a message that firing was going on on Mount Scopus. This was the day when the harvest should have begun, and what had happened appeared to have been the result of an unfortunate combination of accidents. A map reference had been given for the place where the Israeli Police were to position themselves, but the UN observer responsible for Mount Scopus had allowed a printing error (a 3 for a 1) to pass in the letter giving the reference which was sent to the Jordanian authorities, which would have placed the Police 300 yards off instead of 100 yards. All the same, my assistant responsible for the Mount Scopus area, Lt-Colonel M. Stanaway, had met the head of the Jordanian delegation to the MAC, Colonel M. Dahoud, before the harvesting operation began and given him a comprehensive briefing. What happened next was that the harvesting was completed within three quarters of an hour, and the villagers went off. Nobody was quite certain whether they intended to come back again or not, and after a bit the UN observers went away, leaving the Israeli Police where they were. This was a mistake. The observers ought to have maintained contact with the Israeli Police and waited until *they* had gone before leaving themselves. As it was, the Jordanians complained to UNTSO about the continuing presence of the Israelis, and after twenty minutes began shooting. That was another mistake. The Jordanians allowed UNTSO far too little time to do anything about their complaint.

So it was a chain of unfortunate circumstances which led up to the shooting and the UN had to take its share of the blame because of the error over the map reference. The Israeli Press made a tremendous fuss over the affair—three Israeli Police and one Jordanian had been wounded. In the course of a conversation with Eshkol I explained quite frankly what had happened and he seemed to take it calmly. But after this the Israelis adopted a much tougher attitude towards the people of Issawiya, as well as demanding an apology from Jordan.

Because of the accumulation of problems facing UNTSO the Secretary-General decided to send his special representative, P. Spinelli, to Jerusalem. Spinelli, though nominally head of the UN administration in Geneva, had been on what amounted to a one-man mission in the area since 1958. He had an office in Amman, and was a shrewd diplomat as well as an agreeable personality. He came to Jerusalem on 31 January, 1965, with General Rikhye, the Secretary-General's military adviser, and they had ten days of talks with representatives of Israel and Jordan. These may have done something towards a temporary lessening of the tension but produced no lasting result.

Independently of the Spinelli mission, we continued our

efforts to get some relief for the inhabitants of Issawiya, but it was not until 26 May that I managed to arrange an acceptable compromise. It took five months for these villagers to be able to work all their lands again.

It was while we were following up the Mount Scopus shootings, in December, that we found ourselves faced with another problem in the same area. For a long time the UN had engaged in negotiations for the rehabilitation and upkeep of the British War Cemetery on Mount Scopus, in which dead from the First World War are buried. Israel proposed that Israelis should do the necessary work, but this was unacceptable to the Jordanians. It was not until the summer of 1966 that a British working party was able to reach the cemetery. We also had trouble over the road from Jerusalem to Issawiya, which had been allowed to fall into a shocking state of disrepair. The villagers had tried to repair it themselves, but the Israeli Police had stopped them and actually destroyed the work which they had managed to complete. A number of humanitarian organizations volunteered to do the work, but none of them ever received permission from the Israelis to do so.

There were problems, too, connected with the fortnightly Israeli convoys to Mount Scopus, which had to pass through Jordanian territory. Half the Israelis in the Mount Scopus buildings were changed every two weeks. At the end of April the Jordanian authorities objected to one of the people the Israelis wanted to include in the convoy on the grounds that he (a man named Rozen) was a spy. The convoy had to be put off more than once. I had to have several meetings with the Jordanian Prime Minister in Amman and with Kidron in the Israeli Foreign Ministry before the Jordanians finally gave way and left the decision to my judgment. To avoid similar conflicts in the future we worked out an arrangement whereby Israel was to prepare a list of those who were to be in the convoy a week in advance, which would give us time to deal with any possible protests.

The unfortunate villagers of Issawiya also continued to provide us with problems. They were supposed to give four days advance notice of any work they wanted to do in their lands, to say exactly where they would be working, and how many of them would be taking part. But they often failed to do this and UN observers had to stop their activities to avoid the risk of a clash between them and the Israeli Police.

In July, 1966, the villagers gave notice that they intended to start cultivation of a 7-dunum plot known as 'Hassan's field'. I persuaded the villagers to put off cultivation there while I negotiated with Kidron in an effort to get Israeli acceptance, but without success. By September we had sent the Israelis a detailed programme of the cultivation that was to take place, of the numbers that would be involved, and how long it was going to take. But the Israelis refused to accept it. If the villagers did start work, said the Israelis, they reserved to themselves the right to take appropriate counter-measures. So in the end I took the step of myself giving the villagers the go-ahead to start work on 17 September. When the day came Israeli Police emerged from the Hadassah Hospital and the Hebrew University and took up positions designed to intimidate the villagers. An armed patrol was sent backwards and forwards across 'Hassan's field' several times. After a while the villagers withdrew their tractors and the Israeli Police adopted a sort of battle formation in the newly ploughed area. After this incident I took the matter up with Moshe Sasson, who had taken over from Kidron in August as chief of the Armistice Affairs Department in the Israeli Foreign Ministry. He, too, like his predecessor, was an able negotiator and capable of being extremely charming in private. He assured me that, while for security reasons it was essential that patrols in the area must continue, there was no need for me to worry. Certainly the amount of patrolling done by the Israelis diminished, and it is reasonable to suppose that the authorities realized the danger of the case coming before the Security Council, where they would have found themselves on very shaky ground indeed.

But all this time the general escalation of tension was continuing. During June, 1965, Fateh carried out six acts of sabotage against Israel, and for the first time members of the Israeli security forces were wounded. An article in the *Jerusalem Post*, which was clearly officially inspired, said that the army regarded these developments very seriously indeed. In an interview with the *Jewish Chronicle* in London General Rabin announced that Israel was capable of meeting all attacks which might be launched against her by the Arabs and that with the help of her friends she would be able to maintain a balance of force in the Middle East area.

On 27 July, 1965, news came of the receipt by Egypt from the Soviet Union of a considerable number of SAM–2 ground-to-air missiles, to be set up round Suez and Cairo.

One day we received information that the Israelis had been bringing mortars into the Jerusalem area. When we protested we were told the step had been taken for reasons of 'security' and that the mortars would be removed as soon as the situation permitted. Again there was nothing we could do. We had some reason to believe that a similar build-up was taking place on the Jordanian side, though we had no actual confirmation of this. I spent my time commuting between Jerusalem, Amman and Damascus, trying to reduce the tension which was continually building up along the demarcation lines.

During the course of the summer a number of minor acts of sabotage against targets in Israel were carried out. Most of these were pretty amateurish, though inevitably some damage was caused. In the end Israel predictably retaliated. On 5 September, 1965, eleven irrigation installations near Qalqiliya on the West Bank were destroyed, the Israelis claiming that it was from this district that the saboteurs had come. It was, in fact, sometimes possible for us to trace the tracks leading from Jordan into Israel and back again, and at other times we could only trace tracks going into Jordan, which could mean that the saboteurs had entered Israel from somewhere else and made their getaway into Jordan. It was difficult to be certain about all this because we did not have our own trackers or dogs and had to borrow their services from one of the countries involved. UNEF in Gaza for a time had its own dogs and trackers, and I consulted with them about the possibility of getting some for ourselves. But nothing came of it, and after a while UNEF disbanded its dog unit.

In February, 1966, there was a change of Foreign Minister in both Jordan and Israel. In Jordan Hazem Nusseibeh, himself a Palestinian Arab, was dismissed after he had made a speech attacking the PLO and its leader, Ahmed Shukeiry. In Israel Abba Eban took over from Golda Meir. I visited him soon after he had assumed office, and found him already extremely well briefed on the situation—as he had every reason to be, having served for many years as leader of Israel's Delegation to the UN. Eban was a scholar as well as a politician, highly intelligent and an eloquent speaker. He had a thorough mastery of all the business that came his way.

Now followed a relatively peaceful period—though we could not know it, the calm before the storm. HJK–IMAC managed to clear up all the outstanding cases that had been submitted to it.

In March the American Colonel Floyd Johnson turned up to replace Colonel Marsh. From as far back as 1953 it had been a tradition that an officer from the US Marine Corps should be UNTSO's senior military observer, and this had produced a succession of very able officers. But Colonel Johnson had previously served as Military Attaché in Baghdad, which was not an auspicious background for service with UNTSO. Service Attachés, in America as elsewhere, are generally with good reason thought to have links with some intelligence department and, even if Colonel Johnson was innocent of the suspicion, the Arabs assumed that he was working for the Intelligence. This made things harder for us. Relations between Colonel Johnson and the Arab Governments deteriorated, especially following the June War. Thereafter the Syrians boycotted him, and though he was permitted to enter Egypt he was no longer allowed to attend meetings as my deputy. This meant that he effectively ceased to be of any real use to UNTSO.

After several months of inactivity Fateh started up operations against Israel again in April, 1966. Israeli reprisals took the form of attacks against villages north of Jerusalem and in the Hebron area. Several houses were blown up and eight civilians killed. There were heavy exchanges of firing between units of the Israeli and Jordanian armies, particularly around Jenin, in the north of the West Bank, where an Israeli patrol road ran within a few yards of the demarcation line. Then there were other clashes along a patrol road near Khirbit Bitmirsim.

We established mobile observation posts in these areas, which did something to reduce the amount of shooting.

I had long discussions with Israeli officials about their Government's policy of massive reprisals as the answer to acts of sabotage, urging that it would be much better if they reported such acts to the Security Council. As it was, a vicious circle of sabotage, reprisals, and more sabotage was built up, which it was impossible to break. The Israelis insisted that the villages which had been targets for these latest reprisal raids were known hiding places for Fateh units, and said that public opinion was clamorous for revenge.

Discussions kept on coming back to the question of the status quo. But what exactly was the status quo, for example, in Jerusalem? Nobody could really say. In the spring and summer of 1966 we had continuous debates about this, because both Israel and Jordan were keen to find some way of reducing tension between them. But neither side would yield an inch on what it considered its rights, and they both kept on trying to improve their position, which meant altering the status quo in their own favour. If we could have taken up in a sub-committee of HJK–IMAC some of the minor incidents which occurred we could probably have found a peaceful solution to them. But as it was both sides looked on even the most trivial incident as an opportunity for 'establishing facts' in preference to reporting it to us. By the time UNTSO was brought into the picture attitudes would have hardened and a minor incident would be on the way to becoming a major one.

At the end of March Kidron put up a proposal that all military installations between the demarcation lines in the Jerusalem area should be destroyed. There was a certain logic in this, but the Jordanians claimed that these military installations were part of the status quo dating from 1948 and, as there were many more Jordanian than Israeli installations, Jordan would be the loser if the Kidron proposal was adopted.

In June, 1966, I toured the whole length of the demarcation line from the south end of the Dead Sea to the Gulf of Aqaba, partly by car and partly by helicopter. One of the places I visited was the fortress of Masada, built by Herod in 36–30 BC and occupied by Jewish Zealots in their war against the

Romans in AD 66. The Romans had to deploy 15,000 men to overcome the garrison of under 1,000, and were only successful after they had built a sort of huge ramp against the fortress from the west. When they realized that defeat was inevitable all the garrison except for two women and five children committed suicide (AD 73). Masada has come to play a great part in the life and thought of Israelis. All recruits for the Tank Corps are taken to the site, where a torchlight ceremony is held during which they take an oath: 'Masada shall not fall again'. The tradition of the Zealots is not to be underestimated.

New problems continued to crop up in connection with the demilitarized zone between Israel and Syria. In June General Sweidani, who had succeeded General Jedid as Syrian Chief of Staff, made it clear that if the Israelis began cultivating the disputed area in the southern part of the demilitarized zone the Syrians would begin cultivation in the central part. 'We shall not shoot,' he said, 'but if they cultivate, we shall cultivate: we shall exchange land for land.' I called a meeting of my advisers to discuss the matter. We managed to get a week's postponement, which was later extended, so that the matter dragged along towards the beginning of 1967.

In the middle of these negotiations Ralph Bunche came on a visit. He had first been to see the UN forces in Gaza, where I had joined him on 5 July. When we got back to Jerusalem we had a full meeting which included the chairmen of the four MACs and the staff of UNTSO. Bunche told us that the Secretary-General had had several meetings in the spring with the Foreign Minister of Jordan about Fateh activities and had gained the impression that his Government was opposed to these activities, but that owing to the length of the border with Israel and the fact that half the population of Jordan was Palestinian and tended to feel sympathetic towards Fateh there was not a great deal that they could do.

The same day Bunche had a meeting with Eshkol, at which the position of UNEF came up. There had been a good deal of pressure at the UN for a reduction in these forces, largely on the grounds of expense. Some of the great powers, including the Soviet Union and France, refused to contribute to their cost, which put a disproportionately heavy burden on other

Governments. Eshkol stressed the importance of their rôle in keeping the peace along Israel's border with Egypt. So did Eban, whom Bunche saw also. Eban asked him specifically whether, if the other UN forces in Sinai were withdrawn, it would be possible for the UN to maintain its garrison at Sharm el-Shaikh, which guarded access to the port of Eilat. Bunche's answer was that if UNEF had to be withdrawn the Sharm el-Shaikh garrison would have to go too. The same day he saw the Jordanian Foreign Minister.

Between all these meetings Bunche found time to tour the Mount Scopus area and to visit the spot where Count Folke Bernadotte had been murdered in 1948. He mentioned that he ought to have been in the same car with Bernadotte on that occasion, but had been held up so that his place was taken by somebody else. Bunche looked ill during this visit, and had in fact decided to give up his post as Under-Secretary-General. But he allowed U Thant to persuade him to stay on for a further five-year period, and was still serving when he died in 1971. He was a great servant of the UN and a tireless worker for international peace.

In August, 1966, an incident involving Israel and Syria occurred which could have had extremely serious consequences and even have led to a general war. On the morning of 15 August Israeli patrol boats were cruising only about 50 yards off the eastern shore of Lake Tiberias, between OP Delta and OP Foxtrot. There was an exchange of shots between the boats and the shore, but it was difficult for the observers to determine who had fired first. Whatever its origin the firing rapidly escalated. Both sides sent in planes. One of the Israeli boats went aground and a Syrian Mig–17 crashed in the lake after attacking the grounded boat and another Syrian plane was shot down by an Israeli fighter. Eventually the chairman of ISMAC, Captain E. Sparre, managed to get a ceasefire agreed.

The Israelis asked Sparre to help in a rescue operation, and at first it looked as if this would present no difficulty. It also appeared that the Syrians would let the Israelis recover the Syrian plane that had been shot down in the lake, provided the body of the dead pilot was returned to Syria. But then

the Syrians demanded to be allowed to recover the plane themselves, and said that unless they were given this permission
they would not let the Israelis tow away their grounded boat,
for although the boat was in Israeli waters it was within range
of Syrian guns. This the Israelis were unable to concede, and
at a meeting I had with Eban he stated their intention of
going ahead with their own rescue operation, independently
of the Syrians but with the active co-operation of UNTSO.
He wanted UN observers to be positioned between the patrol
boat and the shore, which he thought would discourage the
Syrians from opening fire.

I rejected this plan, as I had no wish to expose my observers
to unnecessary risk. Instead, I asked Eban to accept a delay to
give me time to work out some arrangement acceptable to
both parties. This he agreed to, provided that the delay was
a short one. The proposal I put forward was that Israel should
conduct the rescue operation for the boat—that is, should get
it afloat again—but should have nothing to do with the plane.
Before work on the boat started it should be inspected by UN
observers to see if it had any weapons on board which in-
fringed the armistice agreement. Thereafter the observers
should take up a position between the patrol boat and the
shore in a boat with a white flag. There should be Syrian
observers stationed on the Syrian side while all this was taking
place. This proposal was agreed to by both sides and the
rescue operation began on 25 August. The boat proved to be
fast aground, and it was not until late in the afternoon of the
26th that it was successfully towed off. When this happened
we could all breathe more easily. Later we learned that the
plane had not been left untouched during the eleven days that
had passed since it crashed. There had been a keen contest of
frogmen round it, and the Syrians had managed to get away
with the body of the pilot and several pieces of the plane.

It cannot be doubted that this was an occasion when UNTSO
performed a very valuable function. If Israel had gone ahead
with its own plans for rescue an extremely serious situation
could have arisen. The Syrians would have retaliated by mount-
ing a rescue operation of their own, and then the fat would
have been in the fire. Israel would have felt obliged to

neutralize some of the Syrian positions on the Golan Heights, and perhaps even to occupy part of the Heights. The Arab reaction to such a step would almost certainly have led to war. The stage was set for a first-class row, which by great good fortune was avoided—or, rather, postponed.

CHAPTER 6

COUNTDOWN FOR WAR

✼ ✼ ✼ ✼

Over 13 and 14 July, 1966, there was more guerrilla activity inside Israel; a house was blown up and several people injured. Israel's retaliation took the form of air attacks on workmen and equipment engaged in the diversion of the Hasbani and Baniyas Rivers. I had meetings with the Israeli Foreign Ministry and the Syrian Army Headquarters and appealed to both sides to observe the armistice agreement. For a few days my appeal appeared to have some effect.

In September there were more acts of sabotage. Two members of Fateh were killed and the Israeli Chief of Staff, General Rabin, issued a strong warning to Syria. In October there was another wave of sabotage, including an attack on an Israeli village south of Lake Tiberias. An Israeli Police car, on its way to investigate, ran over a mine and four occupants of the car were killed. This led to a tremendous outcry in the Israeli Press. The Israeli Government called for a meeting of the Security Council and we had to prepare a full report for the Secretary-General. At the Security Council Eban demanded a clear condemnation of Syrian policy, but no resolution was adopted as the Soviet Union exercised its veto. However, as ten members of the Council voted in favour of Israel the Israelis could count this a victory.

It was extremely difficult to say where the perpetrators of many of these acts of sabotage came from, which meant that the chairmen of the MACs often abstained when a vote was taken on a resolution put forward by Israel. UNTSO in consequence became the target for a great deal of criticism from

99

the Israelis, who could not see why we did not 'exercise our judgement' and accept circumstantial evidence. But this we obviously could not do. The MAC could condemn the act of sabotage, but could not go on from that to apportion blame to the Government of the country from which the saboteurs might have come.

The Israeli criticism was directed in particular against the chairman of HJK–IMAC, Colonel Stanaway. But his back was broad and he was able to bear it, and he had full support from me and from the Secretary-General. As Bunche said in a telegram: 'The Chairman is in an exposed position, but what he is taking part in is no beauty competition. He should be told that he has the Secretary-General's full support.' It is interesting to note that Israeli attacks on UNTSO were seldom if ever heard in the course of Security Council debates. During one of these debates the Israeli delegate, Michael Comay, said, 'The armistice machinery was never designed to deal with hit-and-run guerrilla warfare, which is not mentioned in the agreements. The statement made yesterday by the Chairman of HJK–IMAC is virtually a cry of helplessness and frustration at seeing his rôle reduced to that of a Police investigator who has nothing to do but record footprints.' When I pointed out this different treatment to Sasson all he said was: 'These are two different forums.'

On the night of 12 November there was a case of sabotage south of Hebron. The Israelis laid blame on a Jordanian Police Station in the village of Es Samu, a little north of the demarcation line. 'That Police Station is going to be blown up in the next few days,' Colonel Stanaway told his wife, when he heard the news on Israeli radio, and that is exactly what happened. Retaliation came not at night, as was usual, but in broad daylight. Israeli tactics were changing. This time they launched a full-scale attack, probably using a full brigade, of which only one battalion actually crossed the border, the rest remaining in reserve. The assault troops were supported by about twenty armoured vehicles as well as planes.

This was the biggest action since the Sinai campaign of 1956 and lasted for four hours. It took us a long time before we could contact the responsible authorities in Israel in an effort to get the fighting stopped. In the end we were successful, but not before the Israelis had completed the operation to their satisfaction, by which time 125 buildings had been blown up and seventeen people killed. A communiqué was issued which said that the reprisal attack was necessary to demonstrate to Jordan that peace could not be maintained on one side of the border only. There was a considerable reaction to the raid in many quarters. Israel was condemned by the Security Council, and in Jordan there were riots and a curfew had to be imposed. The leader of the PLO, Ahmed Shukeiry, intensified his attacks on King Hussein.

A suggestion made by the Secretary-General in the wake of the Samu attack was that UNTSO should be strengthened. But this was rejected, among others by Israel, which feared that this might mean the creation on its other borders of something on the scale of UNEF—and after 1956 Israel had never allowed any UN troops to be stationed on its side of the Israeli–Egyptian border.

The number of mine explosions inside Israel increased, many occurring on roads close to the demarcation lines. The Israeli troops patrolling these roads often behaved in a provocative manner. Although the Israelis had a perfectly good legal right to build patrol roads a few yards from the border we many times pointed out to them that they could exercise just as effective control if the roads were 50 yards back. Our arguments made no impression. The answer always was: 'We have sovereignty there, and we mean to exercise it'—though once, I must admit, one Israeli official did concede that 'perhaps in 20 or 30 years we may take a different view'.

The first month of 1967 gave a foretaste of what was to come. Warning shots were fired by the Israelis over Arab farmers trying to cultivate lands in the central sector of the demilitarized zone between Israel and Syria, the intention being to prevent the Arabs from entering the Almagor area. The Syrian response was to fire on Israeli farmers in the southern sector of the zone. In the course of the next few days the firing intensified, heavy artillery and armoured cars being brought in. I insisted that this was a flagrant breach of the armistice agreements which had been unconditionally confirmed by both parties on 9 July, 1966. But the military build-up on both sides continued.

As has been shown, the problems of cultivation in the demilitarized zone had been a preoccupation of ISMAC for many years without getting any nearer to a final solution. During the summer and autumn of 1966 we had made a series of fresh attempts to reach some sort of agreement whereby the repeated violations of the armistice agreements could be avoided and at the same time the peasants be allowed to cultivate their lands. Mention has already been made of the outbreaks along the demarcation line in January, 1967, and there is no doubt that most of these had their origin in disputes over the cultivation of the demilitarized zone.

On 15 January, 1967, after receiving a report from us about the situation, the Secretary-General issued another appeal for restraint to both parties. He also urged them to agree to the proposal we had put forward for an immediate meeting of the MAC. Agreement came, and on 25 January the 80th extraordinary emergency meeting of ISMAC was held in a nissen hut by the old customs house on the Syrian side of the Banat Yacub Bridge. The meeting should have been presided over by the Chairman of ISMAC, Captain Sparre, but he had been killed in a car crash a few days before. My deputy, Colonel Johnson, was unacceptable to the Syrians, so that left only me, which meant that my projected sick leave had to be put off indefinitely. (I had had another severe attack of hepatitis at the beginning of December and, though, after a week in hospital I had got back on my feet again, the doctors had strongly advised a couple of months' sick leave.)

The agenda drawn up for the meeting, which was approved by both sides, described its purpose as being 'to find practical solutions to the problems of cultivation along the demarcation lines with a view to creating a peaceful atmosphere for the peasants and other civilians in the area'. Both delegations turned up in full strength, the Israelis led by M. Sasson, and the Syrians by Captain A. Abdallah. The meeting went on a long time, and eventually the Israelis produced their proposals, which were drawn up with deliberate imprecision. These were left over for consideration at the next meeting, which was held

on 29 January at Mahanayim on the Israeli side. After a discussion of the Israeli proposals Captain Abdallah put forward
the Syrian proposals, which contained, among other items,
three points involving the demilitarized zone where the Syrians
refused to recognize the sovereignty claimed by Israel. An
official Israeli statement, issued on 17 January, in which full
sovereignty over the zone was asserted, did nothing to help the
negotiations forward. I tried to get the Syrians to withdraw
these three points on condition that they would come up for
discussion at a subsequent meeting, and suggested that meanwhile we should concentrate strictly on subjects covered by
the agenda. But in this I was unsuccessful. At the next meeting, on 2 February on the Syrian side, both sides took up unyielding positions and introduced a number of fresh topics
outside the agreed agenda. The meeting lasted only a short
time. I continued to negotiate separately with the two sides
till 23 March, when I returned to Norway on sick leave, where
once again I was in the good care of Professor Jervell at Ulleval
Hospital. On 8 April I received a telegram from Bunche saying
that a serious situation was developing along the Israeli–
Syrian demarcation line and asking if I could return quickly.
Professor Jervell wanted me to continue the treatment some time
longer, but on 20 April another urgent telegram came from
Bunche and the next day I was on my way back to Jerusalem.

I found a greatly worsened situation. As long as there had
been any possibility of the negotiations producing some result
the parties had remained relatively calm, but as the negotiations dragged on and the prospect of their producing any
positive result diminished, violence started up again. First the
Syrians opened fire against Israelis who had begun cultivation
in an area where the Syrians thought they had no business to
be. On 2 and 3 April there had been an intense exchange of
fire in the southern sector of the demilitarized zone. Both the
new chairman of ISMAC, Lt-Colonel Bunworth, and my
deputy did their best to get both sides to stop hostilities, but
without success. This was, of course, just the sort of situation
we had hoped that the renewed meeting of ISMAC would
have been able to prevent.

On 7 April there was more firing and on a greatly increased

scale. A large number of aircraft were involved on both sides—
70–80 were reported on the Israeli side and 30 on the Syrian.
Seven Syrian planes were said to have been shot down, and
there were reports of a number of air attacks by Israeli planes
on Syrian villages. On 15 April Colonel Johnson had proposed
that ISMAC should undertake an inspection of the demilitarized zone and of the 'defensive areas'. Syria agreed, on
condition that inspection of the demilitarized zone should
come first and that any military personnel or weapons found
there should be removed. Only after this should inspection of
the 'defensive areas' start. Israel agreed too, but on condition
that the inspection was carried out in the same sequence as
last time. So the inspection never took place. But it is interesting to note that Israel had accepted the idea of an inspection
at a time when a great many rumours were circulating of big
Israeli troop concentrations in the vicinity of the demarcation
line with Syria. UNTSO, which carried out daily patrolling in
the area, had not noticed any such concentrations, but it has to
be remembered that Israel had acquired an almost legendary
ability to mobilize its forces and concentrate them at the right
time and in the right place. It had been estimated that Israel
could mobilize 300,000 men—that is ten per cent of its population—in 48–72 hours. This operation necessarily involved the
country in great economic hardship, which meant that Israel
could not remain mobilized or at war for very long without the
injection of massive aid from outside—all of which calcula-
tions undoubtedly played their part in Israel's decision on 3
June to go to war.

The Soviet Union warned Syria about Israeli troop concentrations and the likelihood of an attack. Nasser gave credence
to these warnings and resolved to support Syria by concentrating Egyptian forces in Sinai, in spite of the fact that his army
and air force were at the time heavily committed in Yemen.
Nasser was obliged to act if his reputation in the Arab world was
not to suffer, because he had been subjected to a lot of criticism
on the ground that he was sheltering behind UNEF. Presumably
his hope was that his gestures of support for Syria would be
sufficient to dissuade the Israelis from attacking Syria.

On my return I again appealed to the parties to keep the

armistice agreement, but at the same time I told them I thought a resumption of negotiations about cultivation in the demilitarized zone should not be resumed until the atmosphere for them was more favourable. The mistrust displayed at the last meeting had shown that for the present there was no possible basis for an agreement.

Israel had already announced that Independence Day (15 May) would be marked by a military parade in Jerusalem, though it was stated that this would not involve forces or armaments in excess of those permitted by the armistice agreements. In spite of this the Jordanian authorities protested, maintaining that such a parade would give Israel political advantages which were contrary to the agreements. Subsequently Jordan lodged a formal complaint with HJK–IMAC. I had several meetings with both Israeli and Jordanian officials but without getting anywhere. I could only hope that there would be no fresh complications.

The Jordanian complaint was heard at a meeting of HJK–IMAC on 14 May, with Colonel Stanaway in the chair, which began at 8 o'clock in the morning. Both my political and military advisers were present, and we hoped that we should be able to get through the agenda fairly quickly. But in this we were to be disappointed. Colonel Dahoud, the chief Jordanian delegate, was drafting a resolution demanding cancellation of the parade, and discussions went on throughout the day and into the night. I was kept continually in touch, and at 1.30 am my legal adviser, Prieto, telephoned to say that no decision had been reached. I told him that if after an hour there was still no agreement he was to let me know and at the same time to arrange for a meeting with the Jordanian Foreign Minister that same night. At 2.30 Prieto rang again to say that a meeting had been arranged for me in Amman at 5 am. After an hour and a half's drive by car, in the course of which I worked out a statement to be made by the chairman of the MAC when it reconvened at 9 am, I met the Foreign Minister, M. A. Toukan. He agreed with the statement and informed me that the Jordanian Chief of Staff had wanted to send troops into East Jerusalem to balance the Israelis on the other side but that he had opposed the idea. This was good news, since such a move would have been bound to increase tension. We were back in Jerusalem by 8 o'clock, the meeting of the MAC took place and the Chairman's statement was approved. The time was by then 9.30. At ten the Israeli military parade began.

＊　　　　＊　　　　＊　　　　＊

Immediately outside the main gate of Government House, which was in no-man's-land and facing towards Israel, there was a small Police hut with a telephone laid on. It was set up as a protection for my predecessor, Von Horn, whose life had been threatened. Originally there had been four telephone lines connected to it, but at the end of April the Israelis increased their number to fifteen. Obviously some large operation was being planned. Israeli civilians and military were continually coming right up to the entrance of our Headquarters in Government House which was a clear violation of the armistice agreements. So UNTSO lodged a protest against both the expansion of the telephone network in the hut and against the patrolling.

It was my custom to spend Norway's National Day, 17 May, with the Norwegian forces which formed part of UNEF in Gaza. But by 1967 the Norwegian–Danish contingent had been withdrawn and replaced by a Swedish battalion, Norway retaining only a field hospital at Rafah, an hour by car from Gaza. My family and I were just about to leave for Rafah on the night of 16 May when we received a telegram from General Rikhye, Commander of UNEF, which effectively put a stop to the idea of any celebration. This was a copy of a telegram which Rikhye had sent to the Secretary-General and contained a warning which he had received from the Egyptian Minister of War, General Mahmoud Fawzi. This warning stated: 'For your information I have given instructions to all UAR armed forces to be ready for action against Israel the moment it might carry out any aggressive action against any Arab country. Due to these instructions our troops are already concentrated in Sinai on our eastern borders. For the sake of the complete security of all UN troops which man observation posts along our borders I request that you issue your orders to withdraw all these troops immediately. I have given my instructions to our commander of the eastern zone concerning this subject. Inform back the fulfilment of this request. Yours, M. Fawzi, Chief of Staff of UAR Armed Forces.' The Egyptian officer who delivered this message to Rikhye had also asked for UN forces to be withdrawn from El Sabha and Sharm el-Shaikh, as Egyptian forces intended to occupy both places that night. General Rikhye's answer had been that he had no authority to comply with these demands, and that a decision must be left to the Secretary-General of the United Nations.

General Rikhye's action was entirely correct, and his conduct in this crisis was most commendable. But in spite of Rikhye's answer Egyptian troops moved in and took over the UN observation post. That same afternoon, 17 May, U Thant had an informal meeting in New York with representatives of countries which had furnished troops for UNEF.

On 18 May the Secretary-General received from Mahmoud Riad, the Egyptian Foreign Minister, a formal demand for the withdrawal of UNEF in as short a time as possible. That same afternoon there was a meeting attended by the Secretary-General, the UNEF Advisory Committee and three representatives of countries with forces belonging to UNEF, at which the Egyptian demand was discussed. Some of the representatives thought the demand should be resisted and that a decision on it could only be taken by the Security Council or the General Assembly. Others felt that there was no alternative but to accede to the demand. The spokesmen for India and Yugoslavia, both countries with contingents in UNEF, said that when a formal demand was made their forces would in any case be withdrawn. No proposal was made to take the matter to the General Assembly. The conclusion of the meeting was that no course was open to the Secretary-General but to accept the Egyptian demand, and with that conclusion I am in complete agreement.

So U Thant told Riad that the demand for the withdrawal of UN forces would be complied with, the troops being withdrawn in an orderly manner over a period of six weeks. At the same time the Secretary-General sent a report to the Security Council and General Assembly. Because of the outbreak of hostilities the withdrawal process was subsequently speeded up, and all UN troops were out of the Gaza strip and Egyptian territory by 17 June.

U Thant's decision—and, as far as I have been able to ascertain he had in this the full support of Bunche—has been often criticized. For example, Abba Eban, in an interview with the BBC on 24 May, said: 'The Secretary-General's decision to agree a hasty withdrawal of UN forces from Sinai and Gaza will go down to history as one of the greatest diplomatic blunders of all time.' It has been said that Hammarskjöld would never have agreed to the demand, but would rather have asked that fresh forces should be flown from Scandinavia and from other countries that were willing, to replace the contingents being removed. But this sort of talk is quite unrealistic. It only has to be remembered that Egyptian permission was needed before any troops could be landed in Egypt, and that by the time the formal request for the withdrawal of UNEF was received (18 May), Egyptian troops had already occupied all UNEF positions. UNEF was neither armed nor deployed to fight the Egyptian Army.

Hammarskjöld had in his time been severely criticized for the agreement he made with Nasser covering the stationing of UN troops on Egyptian territory. This agreement made it quite clear that the troops were there only as a result of special permission granted by Egypt and would have to be withdrawn should Egypt request it. It is worth mentioning in this connection that the original plan had been for UN forces to be stationed on both sides of the demarcation line between Israel and Egypt but that Israel had refused to permit any on its side of the line. Had the original plan been carried out it is quite possible that the 1967 war could have been avoided. Lester Pearson, who played a leading part in getting UNEF established, used to argue that the only choice before Hammarskjöld was the agreement he got or no agreement at all. That, I think, is true.

Egypt's intention was not that UN forces should be completely withdrawn from the area but only from the demarcation line. This was not possible because it would have left them as passive spectators of a war between Israel and Egypt. U Thant's view was that UNEF was where it was to do a job, and that when the job became impossible it had to leave. U Thant suggested to Israel that instead UN forces should be stationed on the Israeli side of the demarcation line, but this the Israelis refused.

Israel reacted to the build-up in Egypt with orders for gradual full mobilization and for the concentration of the bulk of its forces against Egypt. The Secretary-General decided to fly to Cairo for talks with President Nasser. While in the air he learned that Nasser had given orders that the Strait of Tiran was to be closed to Israeli shipping. This greatly aggravated the crisis, since Israel had made no secret of the fact that it regarded freedom of navigation in the Gulf of Aqaba of such vital importance that any interference with it would be a *casus belli*.

At U Thant's request I met him at the airport, and my acting political adviser, the Chinese F. T. Liu, was attached to his secretariat during his stay. At a meeting with Nasser U Thant proposed a moratorium till 10 June to give him time for negotiations with both parties, the great powers, and the Security Council. During this period Israeli ships would not sail through the Strait of Tiran nor would Egypt assert there the rights which it was claiming. Nasser gave U Thant assurances that he would not start offensive action against Israel and would not fight unless Israel attacked first. In view of his heavy commitments in Yemen it does, in fact, seem unlikely that he was contemplating an aggressive war.

U Thant left Cairo on 25 May and next day told the Security Council that the situation in the Middle East was more tense than at any period since 1956. He emphasized that he had had no option but to withdraw UN forces, though if they had been stationed on both sides of the demarcation line the situation would have been different. He repeated the assurances which had been given him by both Nasser and his Foreign Minister that Egypt had no intention of starting offensive operations, but wished to revive the armistice agreement of 1949 which Israel had failed to recognize since 1956 and which should be binding on both parties.

The Secretary-General said that it was not just the closing of the Straits which was responsible for the current crisis;

terrorist activities inside Israel and clashes over cultivation rights in the demilitarized zone between Israel and Syria had played their part also. He concluded by saying that the best hope for a peaceful solution of the crisis was to obtain a breathing space which would give the Security Council time to tackle the underlying causes of the trouble and work towards a political solution. He also took up the question of some form of UN presence in the area, and suggested that for the time being the best arrangement would probably be to re-establish the Egyptian–Israeli MAC (EIMAC) which even then was to a certain extent filling the vacuum left by the withdrawal of UN forces.

First reactions to the Secretary-General's report to the Security Council were positive. Abba Eban, the Israeli Foreign Minister, said at a Press Conference on 30 May, that 'Israel was prepared to wait only days or weeks', and that 'time would be given to the Security Council to find a solution to the crisis'. There were other comments from the Israeli side, including one from Moshe Dayan who had been brought back as Minister of Defence, which seemed to indicate that Israel was prepared to allow the Security Council and the big powers time to do what they could. But it is also possible that these reassuring statements were part of the elaborate preparations for a surprise attack by Israel which were then being perfected.

The Secretary-General's report was first debated by the Security Council on 29 May. The Danish representative, Tabor, who took over presidency of the Council on 1 June, summed up the situation when he said: 'There has been a military build-up along the borders of Israel and the United Arab Republic, and there is no way of denying that the stage is set for a major military clash . . . The slightest miscalculation, the slightest misunderstanding by one or the other side of the opponent's intentions could lead to large-scale hostilities.'*

The Security Council showed support for U Thant's appeal for moderation. The American delegate proposed a resolution in this sense to be debated on 31 May. The debate was postponed, first to 2 June and then to 3 June. There were long

* Quoted in *The UN and the Middle East Crisis, 1967* by Arthur Lall, Columbia University Press, 1968.

discussions about the text of an appeal to both parties, but nothing had been agreed by the time war actually broke out. As the British delegate, Lord Caradon, wrote later: 'Had there not been delay last month, delay in endorsing the Secretary-General's appeal, delay which we strenuously opposed from the first, we might have been able to avert and prevent the war altogether.'*

The whole exercise was a classic example of the failure by the Security Council to reach an agreement, resulting in the Secretary-General getting the blame. But from 18 May, when U Thant received Egypt's demand for the withdrawal of UN forces, until 3 June, the Security Council did virtually nothing. It did not even back up the Secretary-General's report. It appeared scarcely conscious of any sense of responsibility. I often hear criticism of the UN, but my answer is always: 'It is you who are the UN. We are simply its servants.'

The atmosphere at UNTSO headquarters in Government House during these days was fairly normal. Certainly we feared the worst, especially after Nasser's decision to close the Strait of Tiran, but we continued to hope that diplomacy would find a peaceful way out. In the meantime we prepared plans for the evacuation of all UN personnel, not only UNTSO's, in Israel, Lebanon, Syria, Jordan and Egypt, which was a UNTSO responsibility. But work continued normally as far as possible. My family were evacuated to Beirut on 1 June and the same day the observers' families and such members of the staff who could be spared were evacuated also.

We were in continual contact with all Governments in the area. It was agreed that Government House headquarters should be regarded as a sanctuary. This was confirmed after war had actually broken out, and again after fighting had started in the Jerusalem area.

When UNEF was withdrawn we were asked whether UNTSO could take over any of its functions. The Egyptian delegate on EIMAC in particular showed much interest in this, and the Israelis, too, enquired whether EIMAC could continue or even increase its observer services—and this in spite of the fact that Israel had all along been saying it no

* Quoted in Lall, op. cit., p. 68.

longer recognized EIMAC's existence. We made some plans along these lines, including plans to strengthen EIMAC. The Egyptian delegate also suggested that we should take over three of the UNEF camps in Gaza, but higher authority later overruled him.

At the end of May the senior Syrian representative on ISMAC, Captain Abdallah, said he thought war was inevitable, and that therefore the observation posts should be withdrawn. I refused, and we maintained observation along the Israeli–Syrian demarcation line until 6 June. Then, with the help of the Syrian authorities, the observers' families were evacuated, and the observers themselves concentrated in Damascus and Tiberias.

On 25 May Bunche told us that Eban had notified the Americans that Egypt and Syria planned an immediate attack on Israel. He asked if we would report any evidence tending to confirm this. We accordingly investigated, but found nothing to report. However, the whole area was understandably full of rumours at the time.

On 3 June I went to Beirut to see how the evacuation was proceeding and to see my family. My Director of Administration, Dennis Holland, was in Beirut too and said he thought that the danger of a surprise attack had been removed, at any rate for the time being. I felt things had gone so far that it was hard to see how any peaceful solution could be found. I had been optimistic earlier, but the re-shuffling of the Israeli Government on 1 June, with the inclusion of Moshe Dayan as Minister of Defence, had made me change my opinion. After a delay because of engine trouble to our UN plane we took off from Beirut airport in the afternoon of 4 June, landing in Amman because Kolandia airport was closed for repairs. Thus it was that our plane was destroyed on the ground when the airfield at Amman was blitzed by Israeli aircraft on 5 June.*

During our journey to Jerusalem my driver told me that there had been evidence of a great deal of military activity in the Jordan valley that day, but no sign of any troop concentrations in the neighbourhood of Jerusalem.

---

* The plane was replaced by a Fokker Friendship paid for by the Royal Netherlands Air Force, and later by a Dakota from Bell Air paid for by the Swiss Government.

The war starts in Jerusalem. The Jordanian forces opened fire at 11.25 am on 5 June, 1967.

On the terrace of Government House, November, 1967. In front of the Author stands Henri Vigier.

10 On the Israeli-Syrian ceasefire line, March, 1968. In the background to the right is Mount Hermon.

11 Meeting with General Dayan after the Six Day War. Left to Right: Lt-Colonel Hagerty, Y. Tekoah, for many years Israel's Ambassador to the UN, Lt-Colonel S. Gat, General Dayan, the Author, Miguel Marin.

CHAPTER 7

THE SIX DAY WAR

✻ ✻ ✻ ✻

The war broke out early in the morning of 5 June. At 8.30 Pragai rang from the Israeli Foreign Ministry asking me to come round. I suggested meeting him at 10.30, but he said that would be too late as the matter was urgent. So I got into my car and went to the Ministry at once, where I was met by Arthur Lourie who told me that Egyptian planes had taken off against Israel but had been intercepted by Israeli planes. The consequence was that there was now a state of war between Israel and Egypt. Lourie had no further information but asked me to transmit a message to King Hussein expressing the hope of the Israeli Government that he would not join in the war. If he stayed out, Israel would not attack him, but if, on the other hand, he chose to come in, Israel would use against him all the means at its disposal. This was a threat, pure and simple, and it is not the normal practise of the UN to pass on threats from one government to another. But this message seemed so important that we quickly sent it via HJK–IMAC, and King Hussein received the message before 10.30 the same morning.

Back from the Israeli Foreign Ministry we started work. Warnings went out to the Secretary-General in New York, to all our subordinate units, and to General Rikhye in Gaza. Our chief hope was that nothing would start up in Jerusalem, but at 11.25 the Jordanians opened fire. We immediately got in touch with both sides in an attempt to secure a ceasefire, but this was one of the only two occasions—the other being in November, 1956—when our efforts ended in failure. Both sides did, in fact, agree to a ceasefire at noon, but although the scale of the shooting slackened it did not stop. We set a new time limit, and again there was some slackening in the intensity of the fire but no cessation. There was firing on Mount Scopus and round the MAC building. A third deadline for the cease-fire was agreed, but again not respected. We did not, in fact, see a great deal of the fighting. Automatic weapons, artillery, and mortars were used on a considerable scale, but luckily without doing much material damage, and although the MAC building was in the direct line of fire it was not hit. This was fortunate because it was the centre of our communications network, after Government House was taken by Israeli forces on 5 June.

At 1.30 pm I received one of the biggest surprises of my life; Jordanian troops could suddenly be seen entering the Government House area through the gate in the eastern peri-meter. This was the last development I was expecting, since from the military point of view it was impossible that the Jordanian army should try to occupy this area before it had secured Mount Scopus.* I rushed out and met the Jordanian Company Commander halfway between the east gate and Government House and asked him what he thought he was doing. He said he had orders to occupy the area. I told him this was a clear violation of the agreements made between the UN and the Jordanian authorities. The officer, a Major Dahoud, was in command of a reinforced company,† and I made him accompany me to the garage, where I telephoned to the chief Jordanian delegate on the MAC, Colonel Dahoud.

* In *My War with Israel* King Hussein writes: 'General Riad, the Egyptian officer commanding the Jordanian forces, reported "I've given our artillery orders to occupy the front lines, an Infantry battalion of the Imam Ali brigade has been ordered to occupy Mount Scopus in Jerusalem". Mount Scopus is in the demilitarized zone of Jerusalem. The Headquarters of the Norwegian General, Odd Bull, Chief of Staff UN Security Force, has been in this iso-lated spot since the first Israeli–Arab conflict in 1948. Mount Scopus was occupied by our troops a short time later.' But Mount Scopus was *not* occupied by Jordanian troops and UN Headquarters were *not*—and never had been—on Mount Scopus, but on Jebel el-Mukhabbir. Did Israeli intelligence perhaps have a hand in this Jordanian blunder?

† According to King Hussein's book a battalion had been allocated for this task. This might have been sufficient for the occupation of Mount Scopus but quite insufficient for Jebel el-Mukhabbir.

114

He protested that he knew nothing about the order to occupy the area. I made the strongest possible protest and asked the Colonel to get in immediate contact with the Military Commander concerned to get the intruding company removed. But, while I was telephoning, Major Dahoud received an order over his radio that he was to occupy Government House itself.

A good many civilians, including women and children, had not been evacuated and were still in the building. The Major suggested that we should evacuate them but we refused. I took him with me to my office, where I again rang Colonel Dahoud. I do not remember ever having been as angry in my life as when I spoke to him this second time. I told him that if the troops were not withdrawn at once I would make personal contact with King Hussein. This may have impressed the Major, because he, at any rate, thereupon left the building for good. Three Jordanian soldiers had entered Government House with the intention of taking up a position on the roof, but these were stopped by unarmed members of the UN staff, and after a heated argument left the building. When they had left we barricaded the outside gate and all the doors.

But the Jordanian Company was still in the garden of Government House, whence they proceeded to open fire against targets inside Israeli territory. We rang Pragai, in the Israeli Foreign Ministry, and told him of our efforts to get the Jordanian troops removed, and urged on him that Israeli troops should be kept away too. No move coming from the Jordanian side, I tried to get hold of Colonel Dahoud again, but the line was dead. I was not prepared to sit around doing nothing, and was just about to get into my car to go off in search of some responsible Jordanian when the Israeli attack on Government House began with intense firing. So I stayed where I was and at 3.52 Israeli troops occupied UN Headquarters, shooting their way through the solid entrance doors. For the second time in two hours we found ourselves overrun. On this occasion Israel chose to cut our radio link with New York.

The Israelis were convinced that Jordanian troops were still in the building. We assured them that this was not the case, but they refused to believe us and as some of the offices were locked, with a glass partition over the door, they tossed grenades into them to make sure. After this we were ordered to leave in fifteen minutes. That was impossible. There was still a good deal of shooting going on outside, and in addition there were rumours of an impending Jordanian counter-attack. It was in fact 5 pm before we left, and in the meantime several buildings in the Government House compound had been seriously damaged, including a storehouse close to the main headquarters building, hit by over twenty mortar shells, and the flat where my wife and I were living where a fire had broken out. I declined an offer from the Israelis for a lift in their vehicles, and the evacuation of UN personnel took place in UN transport. My own car was one of many which had been destroyed in the attack on headquarters, but I obtained the services of a small private car. The Israelis wanted us to go to Tel Aviv but I insisted on staying in Jerusalem. Essential personnel were lodged in the President Hotel, and about fifty others taken out of the danger area to the village of Ein Karem. I went straight to the Foreign Ministry where for the second time that day I met Lourie, pointing out forcibly to him that we must return to Government House as quickly as possible since this was the centre of our communications network and the only way we had of keeping in touch with the Secretary-General in New York, and with our MACs.

Communications were to remain a problem until we got back to Government House on 24 August. We improvised with such equipment as there was in the MAC building 'between the lines', which was still intact, and with equipment in our vehicles. The first evening we managed to open up a tele-printer link with New York and to contact our out-stations in Amman, Beirut, Damascus and Gaza. We also served as a channel for communications between General Rikhye in Gaza and New York, their regular link having been broken. As far as papers were concerned, my secretary, Pat Ryan, managed to see that the most important documents were brought out with us. In spite of the danger and tension, all our headquarters staff carried out their duties in an exemplary manner. Their behaviour was deserving of high praise.

As time went on we got to know that hostilities had in fact

been started by the Israeli air strike against Egypt on the morning of 5 June. The Egyptian Air Force had been taken by surprise and almost completely put out of action. After this achievement the outcome of the war could not be in doubt; an Israeli victory was purely a matter of time. It is remarkable how, with only a few exceptions, virtually all the Arabs disastrously underestimated Israeli strength. But they should have appreciated that, though small, Israel was a nation in arms, with one of the most highly trained defence forces in the world. Neutral observers in the area never had much doubt who would win if there was another war.

On 7 June we received a telegram from Bunche in which he thanked us for continuing our work in such difficult circumstances. He emphasized the importance of our trying to carry on with UNTSO's normal functions as far as we could, thus providing a continued UN presence in the area, whose services could be available to the combatants if the need arose. He also stressed the need for a speedy return to Government House. As regards the handling of the situation by the Security Council, all he said was that he could have wished for a stronger resolution, but the political situation had not allowed this.

The majority of our observation posts along the demarcation line between Israel and Syria remained manned until 6 June. In OP Delta, at the north end of Lake Tiberias, there were three observers, a Swede, an Italian, and a Canadian. The Sixth of June is Sweden's National Day, and though it was still early in the day the Italian officer, Captain A. Vitiello (who was later to become my adjutant) was just raising his glass in a toast when the Israelis launched an air attack on the post. Two more attacks followed before noon, and at intervals during the rest of the day. Of course we protested, but apparently our protests never reached the Israeli authorities who were convinced that we had evacuated the post on the 5th and that it had been taken over by the Syrians. Fortunately nobody was injured, but part of the trouble may have been that the post was inadequately marked. Learning from experience we were to remedy that defect later. The Delta observers stayed in the post till 4 pm when they were evacuated to Damascus. They met some hostility on the road, but on the whole the evacuation of personnel in Syria went smoothly. The next day an Irish officer, Captain Wickham, who was travelling from Damascus towards Quneitra, was shot and killed by a Syrian soldier. The soldier was later court-martialled and sentenced. But this was the only casualty suffered by UN personnel in the early days of the war. All UNTSO personnel came out of the ordeal with credit, not least those in the HJK–IMAC building, who, under the leadership of Lt-Colonel Stanaway, went calmly on with their work though under cross-fire from both the Israelis and the Jordanians.

The Security Council continued its meeting at 9.30 am on Monday, 5 June—i.e. after war had broken out—but it was thirty-two hours before a weak, but unanimous resolution calling for a ceasefire was passed. (The Soviet Union must be held largely responsible for the delay, because it wanted to combine the call for a ceasefire with condemnation of Israel as the aggressor. In the 1973 war, when there was generally close co-ordination between the superpowers, a resolution simply calling for a ceasefire within twelve hours was passed—and eventually made effective.)

Israel and Jordan accepted the resolution but fighting continued because Israel claimed that Jordan's forces were under Egyptian command.* On 7 June the Security Council passed another unanimous and somewhat stronger resolution, demanding a ceasefire at 8 pm GMT. The following day Egypt accepted the resolution on the condition that Israel did too. In the course of the night 8/9 June Syria followed suit. But still the fighting went on. In such a situation it is not difficult for those who want to continue a war to find excuses for doing so. There is no neutral authority on the spot to enforce a ceasefire. In fact the fighting only stopped as Israel achieved its objectives.

On 9 June, the Security Council passed a still more strongly worded resolution, calling for the fighting to stop immediately and instructing the Secretary-General to get in touch with the Governments of Israel and Syria to ensure that they adhered to the terms of the resolution (fighting had by now stopped on all other fronts). The Secretary-General was instructed to

* Lall, op. cit., p. 61.

report back to the Council in two hours. When he did so, U Thant was able to tell the Council that the Governments of both Israel and Syria had given orders to cease military operations immediately. But at a meeting of the council later in the day he was obliged to report that fighting was still going on and was in fact increasing in intensity. Each side blamed the other, and there were no UN observers on the ground to give the Secretary-General an accurate picture of what was going on.

After a long debate the Council President, Tabor, managed to get agreement to a resolution which included the following passage: 'We call on the parties concerned to extend all possible co-operation to the UN's observers in the discharge of their responsibility; we call on the Government of Israel to restore the use of Government House in Jerusalem to General Odd Bull and to re-establish freedom of movement for UN observers in the area.' So UNTSO was back in business again. Lord Caradon, Britain's Ambassador to the UN, played a leading part in the debate and was successful in reconciling many divergent opinions. He was undoubtedly the outstanding figure in these Security Council debates.

At 4.30 am New York time, which was 11.30 am local time, on 10 June, the Security Council met again at the request of the Syrian Prime Minister, the Israelis having occupied Quneitra on the Golan Heights and being reported moving on Damascus. The atmosphere in the Council was tense, delegates exchanging charges and counter-charges. The Secretary-General quoted reports that Damascus had been bombed, but this was denied by the Israelis—even though a UN observer in Damascus had seen and reported the air attack—and proposed that more observers should be sent to the area. More reports of bombing came in, the Israelis, however, insisting that any of their planes in the Damascus region were only there to give protection to their troops on the ground. This was a clear indication that Israeli troops were now close to the Syrian capital. U Thant also passed on to the Security Council reports from the UN control centre in Tiberias that big clouds of smoke had been seen inside Israel, which suggested that the Syrians were shelling Israeli villages. It was these reports from observers on both sides of the fighting front which helped to direct the course of the Security Council's debates, the Council continually asking for more information from observers on the spot and pressing for UNTSO to be made more effective. As Professor Arthur Lall, who was at that time a member of the Indian delegation, wrote: 'Already in the total UN effort, the Council was but the visible part of the iceberg, the submerged part being persistent UN activity in the field.'*

During the course of the debate the head of the Israeli delegation reported that there had been a meeting between General Dayan and General Bull at which Dayan had indicated that Israel would accept any proposal for the implementation and supervision of a ceasefire. This meeting had in fact taken place at 2 pm local time in the office of the Minister of Defence. After conferring by telephone with my staff in Jerusalem, a ceasefire was called for 1630 hours GMT (1830 hours local time), and both parties agreed. On the whole this time the ceasefire held, though the Soviet Union demanded a fresh meeting of the Security Council on the evening of 10 June on the grounds that Damascus had again been bombed and that fighting continued in the Quneitra area. The Secretary-General produced a report that there had been some bombing 7–10km south of Damascus shortly after the ceasefire was supposed to have gone into effect, and implied that Syrian artillery had also continued to fire on targets in Israel. These violations were not of great significance in the actual war zone though they continued to provide delegates on the Security Council with material for more acrimonious speeches.

The ceasefire came into effect just before sunset, which made it impossible for UN observers to start work until the following day. Because of heavy air attacks and a good deal of helicopter activity in the hours leading up to the ceasefire the Syrians were convinced that the Israelis were planning to continue their assault on Damascus, but in fact there is reason to believe that the Israelis had gone as far as they wanted to. They had secured control of the Golan Heights and of Quneitra, the provincial capital, as well as of the road running from north to south through the area.

On 11 June fresh complaints were lodged with the Security

* Lall, op. cit., p. 84.

Council of Israeli violations of the ceasefire in the south, near Rafid. Israeli troops were also said to have advanced towards the source of the River Yarmuk, one of the main tributaries of the River Jordan. But as UNTSO had no observers in that area it was impossible for us to check. The Israelis denied the charge, insisting that none of their troops had moved forward after 1830 hours on the 10th.

All these developments had meant two hectic nights, those of 10 and 11 June, for all UN staff in Jerusalem, Tiberias and Damascus. Then on 11 June yet another Security Council resolution was voted which condemned all violations of the ceasefire that had taken place the day before. The Secretary-General was asked to continue his enquiries to ascertain whether any violations had in fact taken place and, if it was proved that they had, to ensure that all troops should be withdrawn to the positions they had occupied when the ceasefire came into effect. All parties were instructed to co-operate with UNTSO over executing and controlling the ceasefire. UNTSO would then have the task of determining exactly where the ceasefire lines lay.

Professor Lall's conclusion is that 'The Council had missed its most constructive opportunities when it had failed to act in May, and thereafter it had never really caught up with the flow of events in the region.'* It is easy with hindsight to see what should have been done when the war started on 5 June. The most important task was to establish a ceasefire; everything else could have been left till later. As had happened on 15 July, 1948, when the Security Council ordered a ceasefire, and again on 11 August, 1949, when the Security Council confirmed that order, the Security Council, at its first meeting on 5 June, ought to have passed a simple resolution ordering a ceasefire at a specified time and appointed UN observers to ensure that fighting did in fact stop. On that date all UNEF personnel were still in Gaza and Sinai, except for the Canadian contingent which had been sent home, and could have been used for this purpose. UNTSO had ten observation posts on the demarcation line between Israel and Syria, and most of the observers were only withdrawn on 6 June. They would

* Lall, op. cit., p. 106.

have been in an ideal position to oversee a ceasefire, because at that time there had been very little fighting in this area. HJK–IMAC was also still intact and could have done invaluable work in supervising a ceasefire on its front. If, therefore, the Security Council had taken a rapid initiative, there were UN forces on the spot available to implement it. But, as things actually worked out, Israel had achieved all its military objectives by the time a ceasefire was called for, and it was only on one front, the Syrian, that the UN was able to make any contribution.

Together with representatives of the parties involved UN observers set to work on the morning of 11 June in an effort to trace on maps the ceasefire line. On 14 June the Security Council passed a resolution concerning the security and welfare of the inhabitants of the areas which had been overrun and tried to arrange for the return of refugees who had left the areas. The day before, the Soviet Foreign Minister had proposed in a letter to the Secretary-General the calling of an emergency session of the General Assembly, to meet within twenty-four hours, the purpose of which would be 'to assess the situation that has arisen' and 'to make recommendations to put an end to the consequences of aggression and to effect the immediate withdrawal of Israeli forces behind the demarcation lines of 1949'. The Soviet Union had reason not to be satisfied with the outcome of the Security Council debates, but the General Assembly proved itself hardly more effective. One resolution which the Assembly passed by an overwhelming majority called on Israel to rescind all measures calculated to alter the status of Jerusalem. Israel has continued to ignore this resolution; on 28 June, 1967, the whole Jerusalem area, including the Arab Old City, was incorporated into Israel.

The General Assembly was unable, however, to agree on any resolution pointing towards a political solution for the Middle East. This failure, like that of the Security Council, reflected the disagreement between the superpowers. The Security Council resolutions of 6 and 7 June had stated that a ceasefire should be regarded as the first step towards a political settlement. The world has had to wait a long time for the second step.

122

On 8 and 9 July the Security Council was called upon to consider serious violations of the ceasefire in the Suez Canal area, and this led to the establishment there of a UN observer organization. The Security Council met, following the sinking of the Israeli destroyer *Eilat* on 21 October, and the consequent Israeli reprisals which took the form of destroying Egyptian oil refineries at Suez on 24 October. Both Israel and Egypt demanded a meeting of the Security Council, and on this occasion a serious effort was made to consider 'the next step'—a political solution. After intensive diplomatic activity in New York and elsewhere the famous Resolution 242, which had been drafted by Lord Caradon, was finally voted on and agreed on 22 November—more than five months after the ceasefire had come into effect.*

Meanwhile most of the work falling on the shoulders of UNTSO after the ceasefire of 10 June had been concerned with drawing up the ceasefire lines between Israel and Syria. It was relatively simple as far as the Israeli line was concerned, for the Israelis knew exactly where their forward troops were, and on 15 June a line was drawn on the map and signed by a representative of Israel and by Lt-Colonel Bunworth, the chairman of ISMAC. The line on the Syrian side was harder to determine. As so often happened, the defeated army lacked accurate information as to the whereabouts of many of its units. On 11 June, when UN observers, accompanied by Syrian officers, first went out to discover where the forward units were, they ran straight into an Israeli patrol. The Syrian officers were taken prisoner, but later released as a result of UN intervention. There followed a number of heated discussions in Damascus, the Syrians being in an understandable state of shock after their defeat. But eventually we reached agreement, and on 26 June the Syrian ceasefire line was drawn on the map and signed, though with certain reservations on the part of Syria, by Captain Abdallah and Lt-Colonel Bunworth. Later General Sweidani was to thank us for our help.

Our original hope had been to secure a buffer zone two km wide between the Israeli and Syrian lines, but in this we were not successful. At their narrowest, in the south, the lines were

* Text of resolution in Appendix I.

not more than 300–400 yards apart. Once the lines had been agreed we set up seven observer posts on the Israeli side and nine on the Syrian side. We had ninety observers in this area, who manned the posts in shifts of three to four days. At first the conditions in which they operated were far from comfortable, and they had to live in tents or in lorries which had belonged to UNEF in Gaza. Gradually things improved, we got more equipment, and an operations centre was set up in Quneitra.

After the ceasefire had come into effect we received a welcome telegram from the Secretary-General: 'I convey to you my great appreciation of the initiative and skill you have demonstrated in your ceasefire arrangement in implementation of the Security Council's demand for a ceasefire between Israel and Syria. It is rare, indeed, that a ceasefire can be self-executing. You have provided the intermediary, co-ordination and observance which were essential to bring the ceasefire into reality.'

Negotiations for the return of Government House in Jerusalem as UNTSO's headquarters continued in New York. My staff and I spent only a week in the President Hotel, and then moved to the old YMCA building, one of Jerusalem's landmarks, where we established a telex link with New York, though all our messages had to go *en clair*. After a week there we managed to secure the release of the local Arab members of our staff who had been interned on 5 June. We were now ready to make a fresh start.

CHAPTER 8

REALITY AND PROPAGANDA

The war was over. Israel had won an overwhelming victory. There was rejoicing in the West and millions of dollars and pounds were collected as tribute to the victors. The story of David and Goliath was on everybody's lips—it being forgotten that this was the third time David had felled his giant, each time making his victory more resounding. The Egyptian and Syrian armed forces had lost a large part of their equipment, but the Soviet Union seemed prepared to make good the losses and to supply the defeated countries with the services of her own experts and technicians. In fact, in a fairly short time Egypt and Syria were being supplied by the Soviet Union on a scale far exceeding anything seen before 1967, including the most up-to-date missiles. After De Gaulle had imposed a ban on arms deliveries to Israel as a result of the Six Day War the Israelis turned to the United States to 'maintain the balance of power', and did not turn in vain.

I do not believe that this cycle of arms and counter-arms was inevitable. After the June War the Arabs were in a state of shock, and I am convinced that this offered the opportunity for securing a real peace. Suppose that in the month following the war the Israelis had put their cards on the table and said that, in exchange for recognition, an end to belligerency, navigational rights in the Suez Canal and the Red Sea, and some minor adjustments on the demarcation lines, they were prepared to withdraw from the territories they had just conquered—the Arabs would have received a shock scarcely less profound than that caused by their defeat. It is often argued that the resolution of the Khartoum Conference in August which laid down 'no peace, no negotiations, no recognition' contradicts this assessment, but it should be remembered that on the first day of the Six Day War the Israeli Prime Minister, Levi Eshkol, stated that Israel had no territorial claims, whereas two days later, after the fall of Arab Jerusalem, the Minister of Defence, Moshe Dayan, went to the Wailing Wall and proclaimed: 'We have returned to this most sacred of our shrines, never to part from it again.' At the end of June the annexation of Arab Jerusalem into Israel was announced, and there were many statements in the Israeli press and on Israeli radio to the effect that there could be no return to the armistice demarcation lines of 1949, and that Israel could never withdraw from the Golan Heights, from East Jerusalem, or from Sharm el-Sheikh. It was against the background of such statements that the Khartoum summit took place. These statements gave defeated Arabs grounds for feeling that they had nothing to gain from direct negotiations with Israel—that, on the contrary, Israel would only use negotiations as an opportunity to dictate terms for peace. But the resolutions taken at Khartoum also included the statement that 'the Arab kings and heads of state have agreed to unify their efforts in political action on the international and diplomatic levels to remove the traces of aggression', which implied agreement on the need to find a political solution to the problem. This exactly reflects the atmosphere which I found in all the defeated Arab countries, except perhaps in Syria, after the Six Day War. I got the impression that there was a genuine wish to find a solution to the Arab–Israeli conflict. But, by showing itself unyielding, Israel encouraged the Arabs to adopt a similar attitude. A different approach might have had different results. To my mind this was the best chance of peace in the Middle East there had been since 1949, and it is nothing less than a tragedy that it was missed. Instead of peace there was greater bitterness than ever, and the miserable Palestinian refugees were forced into a new exodus. Until the June War most of them were at least still on the soil of what had been their country, even if living idle in camps; now they were total exiles.

Few people in the outside world appreciated the true situation. When I went back to Norway for Christmas, six months after the war, not one in a hundred of those I talked to had any understanding of the facts. An uncritical acceptance of the Israeli point of view in all its aspects was the rule. Two Norwegian women were exceptions—the authoress Camilla Carlson who wrote an article on the tragedy of Palestinians in *Verdens Gang* on 14 June, and the journalist, Jorunn Johnsen, who wrote a similar article in *Aftenposten* the day after. It required courage to do this, and they found themselves treated practically as 'Enemies of the People'. But I think Ibsen would have been proud of them.

Gradually, it is true, the Norwegian Press shed some of its bias, but for a variety of reasons public opinion in Norway has remained consistently favourable to Israel and unfavourable to the Arabs. In the first place most Norwegians are profoundly ignorant about the politics and problems of the Middle East. Then the Bible naturally disposes them to favour God's chosen people, and their sympathies were profoundly stirred by the appalling fate that befell the Jews of Europe at the hands of the Nazis. Norwegians, like most other Europeans and almost all Americans, found it in no way inappropriate that the Arabs should pay for crimes committed by Hitler.

The West has for a long time preferred to ignore the Arabs or, when this has not been possible, to adopt a severely critical attitude towards them. It was typical that the Balfour Declaration should refer to the Arabs of Palestine—who, after all, at that time represented ninety per cent of the people of the country—as 'the existing non-Jewish population'. The principle of self-determination, on behalf of which the Allies were supposed to be fighting the war, was not to apply to them.

The general disparagement of the Arabs in the West reached its high—or low—point in the mid-fifties at the time of the Suez War. The sort of humour to which we were then subjected is illustrated by the current saying: '*Hitler ist nicht gestorben: er ist nach Egypt gefahren, ins Wasser gefallen, und Nasser geworden.*' (Hitler is not dead: he has gone to Egypt, fallen in the water, and become wet [Nasser].) After the 1967 war propaganda in the West produced endless variations on the theme that Arabs were untrustworthy, stupid, dirty and incapable of agreeing among themselves.

As far as untrustworthiness goes, it is hardly surprising if the Arabs, in view of the treatment they suffered at the hands of the Imperial powers from 1915 onwards, showed a certain lack of trust towards Western policies and intentions. If there is a lack of mutual confidence it is perhaps up to the West to take the first steps towards dispelling it. I remember in 1963, shortly after I had begun my service with UNTSO, and at a time when most of our problems seemed to be connected with Syria, Henri Vigier saying to me: 'If the Syrians come to realise that they can trust you, you will be able to trust them.' In this he proved absolutely correct—and I found his doctrine applied equally well to the other Arab countries, and for the matter of that, to Israel. If I made any agreement with any country I always kept it.

As for the accusation that the Arabs are stupid, all I can say is that I have not found this borne out after nearly eight years of work among them. We had on UNTSO staff about 150 Arabs, mostly Palestinians, who made an excellent impression —hard working and agreeable. I have seen Arabs at work in many other countries and have never had any reason to doubt their efficiency. There is an almost universal eagerness for education. How often have I come across Arabs from impoverished homes where neither parent could read or write who have successfully made their way to a university degree. I recall meeting a young German agriculturalist in Egypt in the summer of 1967 who said: 'If there is any person I have really learned to admire it is the Egyptian fellah. He rises with the sun, works hard all day, and when the sun sets he goes to bed. If he is given advice he is grateful for it and does his best to act on it.'

Cleanliness—I would say that probably Arabs are cleaner than we are. Certainly the religion of most of them—and they are much more conscientious in the practise of their religion than the vast majority of Europeans—enjoins cleanliness upon them.

As for their inability to unite (and Europeans have not themselves shown any conspicuous talent in this direction) it has always to be borne in mind that the so-called Arab world is in fact a patchwork of religious, sectarian and racial minori-

12 *Crossing the Suez Canal, August, 1967.*

13 *The Author with Secretary-General U Thant in New York, 1969.*

14 'It was a miracle that we did not have more casualties.' Suez Canal, 1969.

15 At Nicosia airport, 3 August, 1970; on the way home at the end of the Author's mission to UNTSO. Left to Right: *General Prem Chand*, *Señor Osorio Tafall*, the Author, *Miguel Marin*.

ties. Their differences were open to exploitation, first by the Turks and then by the British, French, and others who took over from the Turks. No doubt today colonialism is officially dead, but outside forces, in the shape of joint stock companies, intelligence agencies, and so on, are vigorously active. In some ways these new alien forces have proved themselves more effective than the old ones—they are more economical in personnel and, because they do not involve the stationing of troops or administrators on the ground, apparently more acceptable to the countries exploited.

The intelligence services of the big powers are, as is well known, used not simply to gather information but also to manipulate political and economic events. In the Middle East, as elsewhere, the CIA and the KGB contend with each other. But it is the Israeli Intelligence Service which is the best and most effective in the area. I remember one of my Israeli friends saying to me: 'We can't afford not to know everything that happens in Lebanon.' And there can be no doubt that they do know. Israeli raids inside Lebanon—like the airport attack in December, 1968, and the commando raid on the headquarters of the Palestinian guerrillas in Beirut in 1973—demonstrated this perfectly. In Syria there was, as has been seen, the example of Elie Cohn and there is reason to believe that others took over after Cohn had been captured and executed.

We in UNTSO saw several examples of the Israeli intelligence machine at work in Jordan. There was, for example, one occasion when the Jordanian authorities arrested two men who were accused of carrying out acts of sabotage in Israel. After further acts of sabotage had occurred, the Israelis informed us, through the MAC, of the names of the saboteurs, telling us that they were the original two who had been arrested, but subsequently released. This could have been bluff but I think it probably was not. It is also difficult to account for the Jordanian attack on Government House in the June War unless Israeli intelligence somehow had a hand in it.

We were given some indication of the extent of Israel's intelligence operations inside Egypt during the exchange of prisoners after the June War, when Israeli agents were among those exchanged. I have also heard Arabs express their belief that the Israelis had infiltrated the Palestine guerrilla organizations, including even the extremist 'Black September'. I used, indeed, to get a feeling that the Israeli intelligence could at times play on its Arab agents as on a well-tuned piano. Whether, as some of my predecessors believed, Israeli intelligence had penetrated UNTSO, it is very difficult to say. They may not have thought it worth their while. After all, we reported everything we did to the Security Council and without the use of a modern coding system. (All our coding work had to be done manually.) They had other ways of keeping track of us.

So much for the popular misconception about the Arabs which I found at home. I must, however, make one exception— the Norwegian Foreign Office appeared to be consistently well informed on Middle Eastern affairs and to have a sensible approach to its problems.

After the June War Israel tried to abrogate all the armistice agreements. The Arab States would not accept this, and in the Secretary-General's report to the General Assembly in September, 1967, he confirmed that the armistice agreements of 1949 were still in force since they could not be unilaterally abrogated. Not, of course, that there was much that could be effectively done as long as Israel refused to co-operate. The agreements went into abeyance, UNTSO's work concentrating on observing and reporting on the two new ceasefire lines, that between Israel and Syria and that along the Suez Canal.

There had been no hostilities between Israel and Lebanon during the June War, though Israeli planes were reported to have flown over Lebanese territory and one of the Lebanese planes which went up to intercept them was said to have been shot down. In spite of this Israel announced that its armistice agreement with Lebanon, as with all its other Arab neighbours, was ended. The only reason I can suggest for this is one episode during the war, when an Israeli member of ILMAC asked for a meeting with a member of the Lebanese delegation. The request was passed on by the chairman of the commission, and a young Lebanese officer to whom he spoke said such a meeting was impossible because Israel and Lebanon were at war.

This message in turn was passed back to the Israelis by the chairman. He was, as I later pointed out to him, wrong to do this since it was no part of our mission to be the channel for messages which could be taken as declarations of war.

CHAPTER 9

THE SUEZ CANAL

�֍ �֍ �֍ �֍

The beginning of July saw a number of violations of the cease-fire with intense firing along the Suez Canal. The Secretary-General pointed out to the Security Council that as there were not observers in the area it was impossible to give an accurate report on the situation or to establish who was responsible for the breach of the ceasefire. In consequence the Security Council unanimously voted on 9 July in favour of setting up a network of observation posts there. This was accepted by both Egypt and Israel. The Secretary-General requested twenty-five new officers for the task, and these, together with seven officers already in the area, formed the nucleus of the Suez Canal Observer Corps.

On 12 July, I had a meeting with General Moshe Dayan, the Israeli Minister of Defence, to discuss the implementation of the Security Council resolution. But before committing his Government he wanted to know what the Egyptians would accept so that conditions on both banks of the Canal should be the same. He intimated that for the time being he was not prepared to give us freedom to patrol between posts on the East Bank. This had been one of the assumptions on which our observer operations were based, and indeed freedom of movement has always been one of the basic principles of UN peace-keeping operations. If we were not to be allowed this freedom we should have to increase the number of our posts. This in the end was what we had to do, but it took time to get all the arrangements made. Dayan agreed that we should carry out a reconnaissance the following day (13 July) on the East Bank of the Canal for an appreciation of our needs in connec-

132

tion with the exercise—numbers, siting, communications, etc.

The same day I flew to Cairo for consultation with the Secretary of State at the Egyptian Foreign Ministry, Salah Gohar, who from now on was to be my Egyptian contact. He had been a General in the army in Gaza and had experience of the working of the armistice machinery and, though difficult to deal with on the official level, he was always personally most charming. My negotiations in Cairo took a long time. The Egyptians were still in a state of shock following their defeat, and extremely suspicious. They refused to allow the use of radio for communication between the observation posts and the UN communications centre, suggesting instead that we should use the Egyptian military network and that the observation posts should report through it to a UN centre at Ismailia which would report back to Cairo and from Cairo to UNTSO headquarters in Jerusalem.* They also insisted that the UN's operations on either side of the Canal should be kept separate from each other and that there should be no direct communication between them.

The Egyptian requirements were completely unacceptable to the UN, it being absolutely essential for us to have our own communications system. We had, of course, kept New York continuously informed of the progress of our talks, and Bunche agreed that we must continue to insist on an independent communications system, though without going so far as to break off negotiations. We had in any case no intention of doing this. We were simply carrying out instructions given us by the Security Council, and if these proved impossible to implement we should have to refer the matter back to the Council. If we were to be unable to transmit messages backwards and forwards over the Canal between posts, and, even more important, between the posts and the operations centre, it would be virtually impossible for us to arrange for the restoration of the ceasefire after a violation had taken place. I emphasized this point at meetings with Gohar and Mahmoud

* Possibly the fact that UNTSO's former headquarters were in no-man's-land in Jerusalem, which have now been declared part of Israeli territory, added to Egyptian suspicion.

Riad, the Foreign Minister, on the 13th and 14th. On the 14th Gohar agreed to allow us the use of radio on the West Bank of the Canal, but still refused to allow communication across the Canal. Nor would he sanction the use of code.

Immediately following this second meeting I flew to Tel Aviv, where Dayan gave approval for four observers and their equipment to go to the East Bank as an advance party. It was also agreed that there were to be sixteen observers on either side of the Canal, though Dayan still vetoed the idea of any patrolling. He also wanted the ceasefire line along the Canal to be marked on a map in the same way that the line between Israel and Syria had been. This, we knew, was something the Egyptians would not agree to for political reasons. Not that it was a matter of great importance, since the Canal itself was the effective ceasefire line between the two armies, except in its extreme northern sector where for about nine km south of Port Said Egypt was in control of both sides.

On 15 July I flew to Cairo with four observers and an ancillary staff who were to form the advance party for operations on the West Bank. When we landed we were told by our Liaison Officer in Cairo, the Italian Colonel di Stefano, that a convoy was waiting to drive the party out to the Canal, the Egyptian authorities being apparently interested in getting us down to work as soon as possible. No sooner, however, had the party, led by the Swedish Lt-Colonel O. Rosenius, reached Ismailia than it was met by intense Israeli artillery fire. On the other side a group of observers led by the Australian Major Roy Skinner, which had reached El Kantara,* was greeted with a low-level air attack by Egyptian planes. Major A. Vitiello, who was himself a pilot and had been exposed to several Israeli air attacks as an occupant of the OP Delta on 6 June, said this attack was very well carried out.

The exchange of fire across the Canal was a severe one. I received a message from Bunche to the effect that Israel was willing for a restoration of the ceasefire if Egypt would agree too. I took this up with Gohar and our Headquarters in Jeru-

---

* Kantara means a bridge in Arabic, and the town is a bridge not only across the Suez Canal but also between Africa and Asia.

salem. The result of this interesting three-way operation—New York, Cairo, Jerusalem—was a ceasefire at midnight.

The following day Gohar repeated Egypt's refusal to allow any direct communications over the Canal or any use of code, and he introduced a new condition—that there should be an Egyptian radio officer in our radio room. I could only report to Bunche that these restrictions would make it impossible for us to carry out the duties with which we had been charged by the Security Council. Bunche agreed. The Secretary-General sent a personal appeal to the Egyptian authorities to withdraw their demands for having one of their own officers in our radio room and a ban on the use of code. Meanwhile I was obliged to inform all concerned that the start of the operation would have to be postponed, and flew back to Jerusalem feeling extremely pessimistic. I happened that afternoon to meet the Editor of the *Jerusalem Post*, Ted Lourie, who asked me when I thought the UN operation was going to begin. I said 'tomorrow afternoon', but without much conviction. The next morning I got a telegram from Gohar withdrawing the demand for their own radio officer but repeating the ban on the use of code.

In these circumstances Bunche agreed that the operation should start on 17 July at 1600 hours GMT. In fact the use of code was never sanctioned by the Egyptians, but after a while they permitted direct communications between operational centres on either bank of the Canal, particularly when it was a question of restoring the ceasefire. That was a considerable help. Also, after a while, limited UN patrolling was permitted by both the Egyptians and the Israelis. So it was that our operation began with only the minimum of the conditions we had set being met. Even so, they proved effective, and the Canal zone became for the time being relatively peaceful.

When the operation began on 17 July the problem of the Canal itself was still unsettled. The Egyptians maintained that as they held full sovereignty over the Canal the Israelis could not make any use of it. On their side, the Israelis claimed that they had had boats on the Canal when the ceasefire came into effect and argued that they should be able to sail these boats in the eastern half of the Canal. It took two weeks and a number of meetings to resolve this problem, Gohar proving a particularly stubborn negotiator. It proved in fact not possible to get the parties to agree, but in the end they both accepted a formula which I had worked out. On 27 July I sent identical letters to the Egyptian and Israeli authorities proposing that all military activity in the Canal, as well as all movements into the Canal by boats, floats, rafts and so forth should cease for a period of one month from 0800 hours that day. The Suez Canal Authority would be permitted to continue supplying the ships which had been stranded in the Canal because of the war. This was to be done solely in consequence of the ceasefire and without prejudice to the political, legal or any other considerations affecting either party. Israel accepted this proposal, but Egypt wanted fresh negotiations on it, which were not concluded until 1 August.

For our part, we would have liked to have at least two UN patrol boats on the Canal, one to operate from Ismalia northwards and one south towards Suez. These would have been useful more for keeping the observation posts supplied and for relieving observers than for taking note of any activity there might have been by either side in the Canal. But we were never allowed to have them.

On 27 August the agreement was extended indefinitely. One difficulty on the Egyptian side was that they had a number of fishing boats in the Canal, most of them in a small harbour one km north of Suez, but eventually they were catered for too. Following a local unofficial understanding with the Israelis they sailed out into the Red Sea. In all it took us three weeks to implement on the ground the Security Council resolution.

I paid my first visit to the observation posts on the West Bank of the Canal on 22 July. Colonel Rosenius had established an operations headquarters in the Suez Canal Authority's Rest House in Ismailia. This had originally been built for the Empress Eugénie on the occasion of the opening of the Canal and suited our purposes admirably. Now the UN flag was flying over the building and our staff had got down to work in a businesslike fashion. From Ismailia I drove south to the Great Bitter Lake, visiting observation posts on the way, and could not help noticing how vulnerable our posts and patrols would be in the event of any exchange of fire across the Canal—something they were in fact to have a good deal of experience of later. In the Great Bitter Lake were thirteen stranded ships belonging to Bulgaria, Czechoslovakia, Great Britain, France, Poland, Sweden and West Germany.

The country on the two sides of the Suez Canal is very dissimilar: on the west it is for the most part fertile, with three large towns strung along it—Suez at the south end of the Canal, Ismailia in the middle, and Port Said at the north end. There is a metalled road all along the West Bank and almost all the installations for the control and administration of the Canal are to be found on this side too. The East Bank is part of the Sinai Desert. At the time of the June War there was little or no cultivation here, though ambitious plans had been made for irrigating this bank with Nile water piped across the Canal. There was a metalled road from El Kantara southwards, but north of El Kantara there was no proper road, though there was a sandy track that could take ordinary transport. A bit to the east of this track was loose sand which could not bear the weight of untracked vehicles.

Most of the length of the Canal on its eastern side was a high bank of sand, thrown up when the Canal was being built, and it was on top of this that we stationed most of our observation posts. To begin with they were housed in lorries taken over from UNEF in Gaza, but as these were gradually shot to pieces we replaced them with caravans, which were positioned on the reverse slope of the sand bank, so that their occupants were at any rate protected against small arms fire from the Egyptian side of the Canal.

At the beginning of August I had a meeting with General Dayan and with the officer with whom we were now to liaise, Colonel Dov Sion, who was also Dayan's son-in-law. I found Dayan, as always, a straightforward person to deal with. He knew exactly what he wanted, and if he made an agreement he stuck to it. On this occasion he said he had received reports that several Egyptian boats had been seen making their way along the Canal from Port Said towards El Kantara. Our observers had not seen this, so probably the movement had been confined to the most northerly section of the Canal where the Egyptians were in control of both banks. On 12 August U Thant asked for the number of observers along the Canal to be increased to fifty, and later in the autumn the total was brought up to ninety.

In the middle of August I went to Damascus to see General Sweidani, now Minister of Defence, and found him a good deal calmer than he had been in the first shock of defeat. He complained that the Israelis had been blowing up houses east of the ceasefire line. The Israeli explanation was that the houses had to be destroyed because their sanitary state was a menace to health. Sweidani also enquired whether Syrian peasants would be allowed to cultivate in the buffer zone between the two ceasefire lines. Israel was against this on security grounds—with good reason, as later events were to show, since the zone was made use of by groups of infiltrators.

On 24 August we moved back to Government House, though we found that the Israelis had built a new fence which restricted the area round the building to a third of what it had previously been. Our main radio mast was now outside the UN perimeter, and not long after we were back an attempt was made to sabotage it—which would hardly have happened if it had been still inside the fence. The sabotage, which the Israelis blamed on the Arabs, was very amateurishly done, as the mast simply fell down without breaking any of the wires. Everything was in working order again within twenty-four hours. As far as I could tell most of our equipment and possessions in Government House were much as we had left them. We had managed, as has been mentioned, to evacuate the most important files, and some personal papers and objects I had sent for safe keeping to the Norwegian Embassy in Tel Aviv or to MAC Headquarters in Beirut.

We found that our bedu dog, Kicki, and our cat, Tutmoses, whom we had been obliged to leave behind when we were forced out of Government House, had now become good friends. Previously they had literally led a cat and dog life together, but the common experience of war had brought them together.

On 28 August I made my first inspection of the East Bank of the Canal. We drove from Gaza to El Kantara, which was the UN operations centre for the East Bank. There were still about 1,200 Egyptians on this bank who wanted to be evacuated to avoid having to live under Israeli occupation, and this we were able to arrange. I visited all our observation posts and then crossed over the Canal—for the first and only time as it turned out. We crossed in an Egyptian boat flying the UN flag and under the command of a Burmese naval officer, but later I got a message from the Israelis that if I wanted to cross the Canal in future next time I would have to use an Israeli boat. As there were no Israeli boats in the Canal at that time this was tantamount to an Israeli veto on a direct crossing of the Canal.

At El Kantara (West) I was greeted by Lt-Colonel Rosenius, with whom I drove north, visiting our observation posts on that side and Port Said, where there were two Russian cruisers in the harbour, presumably acting as a sort of guarantee for Egypt. From Port Said we turned south to our operations centre at Ismailia; then on to Suez, and so back to Cairo.

On the drive to Suez I was struck once again by how vulnerable our observation posts were, and so I gave instructions that all observers must be provided with shelters. The Egyptians and Israelis raised no objections. As a measure of personal protection most observers had already taken to wearing Egyptian steel helmets which they had picked up in the desert. We asked the Secretary-General to authorize the issue of helmets and splinter-proof vests to observers. At first he was reluctant to do this, on the grounds that this had never been done before, but eventually he agreed.

Rosenius on the West Bank and Skinner on the East Bank had done an outstanding job in connection with the setting up of our operations. My Director of Administration, Dennis Holland, quickly provided the necessary equipment for the posts and communications centres at Ismailia and El Kantara. The operation was underway.

The Fourth of September saw the first serious incident since we had arrived in the Canal zone on 15 July. Observers at Port Tewfiq, opposite Suez, reported three explosions but without being able to determine their place of origin. An Egyptian officer explained that it was firing practice. A little while later two Israeli torpedo-boats and a landing-craft were seen about three km south of Port Tewfiq, and another Egyptian officer warned that they would be fired on if they passed north of a line which was later defined by Gohar as latitude 29° 52′ north. Shots were registered falling about 100 metres in front of the three boats, which changed course. Eight minutes later the Israelis retaliated by shelling Port Tewfiq and Suez. Firing gradually spread north along the whole length of the Canal and it was 1605 hours before we managed to stop it, our original call having been for a ceasefire at 1215 hours. Both sides complained to the Security Council, the Egyptians claiming that 42 civilians had been killed and 161 injured and several boats in the Gulf of Suez sunk.

Later the same day I saw Dayan who insisted that they must have contact by sea with their forces at the southern end of the Suez Canal. The Egyptians countered that the Canal authorities had always exercised control two nautical miles from the southern exist of the Canal, and repeated their warning that any ships which entered this space would be fired on. Gohar said that there could be no question of a compromise over this because Suez was a major port as well as the base for a fishing fleet. These two points of view were reported to U Thant who advised Israel not to insist on maintaining contact by sea. It must be presumed that the United States Government put pressure on Israel over this, for though there was never any official change in the Israelis' attitude they never again tried to force their ships into the Gulf of Suez.

After this, firing in the Canal area was fairly frequent, though not on the scale which was to develop later. The Egyptians would open fire on Israeli fighter aircraft, and though these usually kept to the East Bank they were even so dangerously close to Egyptian positions, while the Israelis would fire on Egyptians trying to get their ships out of the Canal. The most trivial incident could lead to a violation of the ceasefire. For example, the Israelis put one of their flags on a buoy which marked the eastern channel at the entrance to the Suez Canal. This the Egyptians regarded as a provocative act, and it took an enormous diplomatic exercise before we could get it removed.

In the middle of August I had a meeting with the Foreign Minister of Jordan, Adib Aamiri, in which we discussed the setting up of observation posts along the ceasefire line between Jordan and Israel. Colonel Dahoud was also present, since there had recently been some firing and violations of the ceasefire in the Jordan valley. The view of the Minister was that this step was not necessary for the present, but he agreed that the chairman of HJK–IMAC, Lt-Colonel M. Stanaway, should become UNTSO Liaison Officer in Amman. The Foreign Minister emphasized the need for an early political solution. This was a matter of greater importance for Jordan than for any other country which had taken part in the recent war, because the Jordanians had lost more than anyone else, and were in an impossible political and economic situation, with the most productive part of the kingdom—the West Bank and Jerusalem—in enemy hands and with a fresh flood of refugees in the East Bank. The need for a political solution was a subject which cropped up in all the conversations I had in Amman. That same day, when I lunched with Colonel Dahoud, he reverted to it, and added that the Israelis were always talking about the need for peace but he thought that they spelt it wrong—what they really meant surely was 'piece', because they had been taking over Jordan piece by piece ever since 1948.

In August the Syrian Government asked for the removal from Damascus of all American personnel serving with the UN, on the grounds that the United States had consistently supported Israel. Later there came a request that Canadian personnel should be removed too, but we managed later to get them brought back, though as long as I was Chief of Staff the ban on Americans remained. This meant that American officers could only serve at UNTSO Headquarters in Jerusalem or in observation posts on the Israeli side of the ceasefire line. This was unfortunate because there was always a danger that, if confined to one side, observers would become partisans, though in fact this never happened and the Americans continued to observe objectively.

In the middle of September I took a holiday. I had been obliged to cut short my sick leave in January and had only had a short break in April. It had been an exacting summer. We were in the middle, too, of changing political advisers; Henri Vigier (though he did not finally retire until the following year) being in process of handing over to his successor, Miguel A. Marin.

Henri Vigier was without question the most valuable member of my staff. He was a scholar by training and temperament, and was one of those whose experience as a combatant in the First World War had taught that war solved nothing and who had subsequently dedicated their lives and talents to the cause of peace. Vigier took a job with the League of Nations and after several difficult assignments achieved the reputation of being one of the League's most effective officials. He remained in Geneva until after the Second World War when he offered his services to the League's successor, the United Nations, even though he had already passed the retiring age. He was attached to the first UN Commission of Enquiry on Palestine in 1947 and was Bunche's principal aide in the 1949 armistice negotiations between Israel and Lebanon and Israel and Syria. Nobody knew the background to the whole situation better than he did, and as long as the armistice agreements continued to function—till the June War, that is—his advice was indispensable. By that time his health had already begun deteriorating, but he never relaxed, and through the difficult hours at Government House on 5 June he was a tower of strength. In May, 1968, he became so ill that he was obliged to stop work, and before he left he was presented with a special address from the Secretary-General, who referred to him as 'an outstanding international official'. All those connected with UNTSO owed much to this remarkable man.

I was planning at one time to put his name forward for the Nehru Peace Prize, and Bunche was prepared to support me. But when U Thant was nominated for the Prize (which he later received) we were advised not to go ahead with our candidate. But I still feel that a man like Henri Vigier, who worked devotedly in the cause for peace for forty-seven years, is at least as worthy of a peace prize as some of the politicians who have won them and who may simply have attracted attention by being in the right place at the right time.

Miguel A. Marin is a lawyer by training who became the legal adviser to the Foreign Ministry of the (Republican) Spanish Government. He was many times Spain's delegate to the League of Nations and was fond of recalling that in the Fourth Committee, of which he was a member, there were two voices raised against Hitler's Anschluss with Austria—his and that of C. J Hambro, President of the Norwegian Storting. After Franco's triumph he left Spain and went to France. One day he was walking down the Champs Elysées when he heard his name called—it was Hambro who had seen him from the taxi he was in. Hambro urged him to start a new life in Oslo, but Marin had already decided to go to Mexico, although he never forgot this gesture by his Norwegian friend. In Mexico he had a successful career as legal adviser to the Government and as Professor of International Law at the National University. In 1946 Trygve Lie asked him to become a member of the UN Secretariat, and he has remained with the UN ever since, eventually becoming head of the Political Division. For a time he was legal adviser to the UN commission for India and Pakistan which was brought into being in 1948 to deal with the Kashmir problem.

The first test for Marin after he joined UNTSO was connected with the setting up of an observer organization on both sides of the Suez Canal. As has been seen, this led to protracted and difficult negotiations. Often, when these seemed to be hopelessly bogged down, Marin would produce a witty remark or a funny story which would lighten the atmosphere and enable talks to be resumed. He did not spare himself the performance of his duties. I found him a true friend and a most valued colleague. I understand that my successor, General Ensio Siilasvuo, has an equally high opinion of him.

On 21 September I received a telegram from Bunche asking if I could cut short my holiday and go to Cairo to see Gohar. I did, and had a meeting with him at the Egyptian Foreign Ministry on 23 September, when I proposed that we should try to improve the observer machinery and try also to find some way of avoiding the continuous outbreaks of firing, often sparked off by the most insignificant incidents. The proposal was that as soon as one or other side (or both) believed there

143

had been a violation of the ceasefire it should make contact with the officer in charge at one of the control centres (Ismailia or El Kantara). After consultation Gohar was prepared to agree in principle with the proposals. A few days later I put it to Dayan in Jerusalem, and the result was a few weeks of comparative peace along the Canal. On 29 September I was able to continue my holiday in Norway.

On my way back from holiday I stopped off in Beirut, where the Chief of Staff of the Lebanese Defence Forces, General Boustany, had asked to see me. A number of acts of sabotage had been carried out inside Israel by infiltrators from across the Lebanese border. He wanted more UN observers in Lebanon as a precaution against Israeli reprisals. This would have required Security Council agreement, but for some reason it was never raised there, and the consequence was that acts of sabotage multiplied, to be followed in due course by Israeli reprisal raids against what they claimed were guerrilla bases.

On 7 October the Finnish Colonel Siilasvuo joined UNTSO. He had been one of the observers in the Lebanon operation in 1958, when he had done an excellent job, and had subsequently been a company commander with UNEF in Gaza as well as commander of the Finnish contingent with the UN forces in Cyprus. I had particularly asked for his services for UNTSO because the presence of such an experienced officer would take some of the work off my shoulders.

CHAPTER 10

MORE TROUBLE IN EGYPT

The Twenty-first of October was another day of dangerous crisis. The Ismailia centre reported, via an Egyptian liaison officer, that an Israeli ship had entered Egyptian territorial waters, had opened fire, and that the Egyptians had returned her fire. A little later, at 1617 hours, we received news that the ship, the destroyer *Eilat*, had been sunk. Shortly after this Colonel Sion informed us that the Israeli Navy and Air Force had begun a rescue operation and asked us to ensure that this was not interfered with by the Egyptians. We immediately passed on this message. Later Sion told us that the *Eilat* had been hit twice by missiles when it was about thirteen miles east of Port Said and about ten miles from land. So we were faced with two completely contradictory versions of what had happened. We had no means of telling where the ship had been when it was fired on, since it could have moved position before it sank; nor could we tell whether the *Eilat* had in fact been the first to fire. The Israeli authorities wanted us to send someone in one of their helicopters to determine the *Eilat*'s position but, in view of our experience over the Mount Scopus convoy and such like, I declined the offer. The only effective investigation would be one conducted by our own people in a vessel flying the UN flag.

After the ceasefire in June there had been a certain amount of naval activity outside Port Said, especially following the numerous violations of the ceasefire at the beginning of July. On 12 July the *Jerusalem Post* reported that the *Eilat* had encountered three Egyptian torpedo-boats and had sunk two of them. In September another clash between Egyptian and

Israeli naval units—an Israeli destroyer against two Egyptian torpedo-boats—was reported in the same area. All these incidents were clear violations of the ceasefire, and even though they took place beyond the area of our responsibility we could have investigated them, if the parties had been prepared for us to do so. Alternatively, the Egyptians could have asked us to pass on a message to the Israelis, warning them that if any of their naval vessels penetrated Egyptian territorial waters they would be fired on, in the same way that we had managed to defuse the trouble that had blown up in the waters outside Suez and Port Tewfiq. Had we been asked to do this the loss of the *Eilat* and the consequent Israeli reprisals might have been avoided.

We had little doubt that the reprisals would come. Moshe Dayan was quoted in the *Jerusalem Post* as saying that the sinking of the *Eilat* meant a resumption of hostilities. Around midday on 24 October—which happens to be UN Day*—there were reports of shooting in the Canal area. We called for a ceasefire effective from 1330 hours, but the Israelis claimed that their communications had broken down and they could only agree to a ceasefire two hours later, at 1530 hours. Their intention was obviously to continue an operation which was meant to avenge the *Eilat*. Further representations by us were unavailing, and the outcome was that the refineries south of Suez were destroyed and the towns of Suez and Port Tewfiq severely damaged. Eighteen people had been reported killed, forty-five wounded, and thirty-six missing when the *Eilat* was sunk. How many dead and wounded there were as a result of the Israeli retaliation it is impossible to tell.

The Security Council quickly got into action and passed a resolution condemning all violations of the ceasefire. One result was that the number of observation posts was increased to nine

---

* UN Day was always celebrated by the Israelis in Jerusalem, even after the 1967 war. There would be a morning ceremony outside the Mayor's office, at which the UN flag would be hoisted. The Mayor or his deputy would make a speech and the official in charge of the UN Development Programme would also make a speech. In my first year of office (1964) I was asked by Kidron if I would officiate, but I explained that this was out of the question, and he agreed.

on each bank of the canal and the number of observers to 90. The proposal to set up an observation post in Port Said was rejected by the Egyptians, presumably because they did not want witnesses of Russian naval activity in that port—though UN personnel continued to be able to go on leave there. The Secretary-General also proposed that we should be equipped with four patrol boats, four helicopters and direct communications across the Canal with the use of code. That both parties should object to the use of helicopters was understandable, but it was disappointing that they were equally opposed to our having our own patrol boats. This would have in no way affected the security of either Egypt or Israel. Nor did we get anywhere in the matter of communications.

So far the countries providing observers in the Canal area had been Burma, Finland, France and Sweden.* Now we had to widen the net, and additional officers were supplied by Chile, Eire, Austria and Argentina, all of whose governments were acceptable to both sides. Egypt made an additional stipulation that they would accept no observers on the West Bank of the Canal who had previously served in Israel, except those who had been on UNTSO Headquarters staff in Jerusalem.

That autumn there was a certain amount of shooting in the Jordan Valley, but as we had no observers there we could not give any accurate report of our own as to what had happened, though we recorded such information as we were able to get hold of. The Jordanians were obviously concerned about the possibility of Israeli reprisals, and during some exchanges towards the end of November Israel sent in aircraft, killing a large number of civilians. We managed on this occasion to secure a ceasefire.

On 26 November the *Jerusalem Post* reported that four new kibbutzes had been established in occupied territory. The same issue carried extracts from an article in *Le Figaro* which alleged that a good deal of brutality had been used in the eviction of Arab villagers from their homes. There can certainly be no doubt that many thousands of Arabs at this time fled across the Jordan to the East Bank, even though there may

* For a time also Australia.

be no precise evidence of the methods that were employed to ensure their departure.

*   *   *

The Security Council Resolution of 22 November laid down that the Secretary-General should nominate a special representative to get in touch with the governments concerned with the aim of working towards a peaceful solution of the conflict. Sweden's Ambassador in Moscow, Dr Gunnar Jarring, was chosen for the task. I was to have regular meetings with him and formed a high opinion of his abilities. He has been much criticized, but obviously one man can do little towards a solution of this most complex of all problems unless he has both the full backing of the big powers and the co-operation of the parties directly involved. His function was supposed to be that of an intermediary rather than a mediator, such as Count Bernadotte had been. I do not think that as such anyone could have done better that Dr Jarring, who worthily carried on the great tradition of Bernadotte and Hammarskjöld.

At my first meeting with Jarring he informed me that he would do his best to secure the release of the ships which had been stranded in the Canal as a result of the June War. Naturally, both the owners of the ships and the insurance companies had been exerting a great deal of pressure on the Governments of Egypt and Israel and on the Secretary-General to secure this. It was felt that if the ships' release could be effected it would improve the atmosphere for the political settlement which Jarring was supposed to be preparing the way for.

On New Year's Eve, when I was at home in Norway, I received a telegram from Bunche telling me that I should have to go back to the Middle East shortly. In fact it did not prove necessary for me to return until 19 January, when I flew to Nicosia where I met Jarring. He brought me up to date with the progress of his negotiations and informed me that the Egyptians had expressed their willingness to allow the stranded ships to be evacuated southwards, under the auspices of the Suez Canal Authority. The Israelis had already agreed on 27 December to evacuation southwards as a one-time operation. But at a meeting with Jarring on 19 January Mahmoud Riad declared that it would be necessary for the Egyptians to make a reconnaissance of the northern part of the Canal before the ships could be moved.

This introduced an entirely new element into the problem, and we could see that it was going to complicate our work, which was essentially to act as co-ordinators for negotiations between the parties. When the actual evacuation began, our rôle would be to provide observers who could follow each stage of the operation and report any violations of the cease-fire. The Egyptians had made it clear that any attempt by the Israelis to interfere with the operation would result in its being halted.

Our negotiations with the Israeli authorities were unsuccessful. They asserted that their consent only covered evacuation of the ships southwards, and that if any complications arose in the course of the operation these would have to be the subject of further negotiations. The presence of Russian warships in Port Said harbour was probably a contributory factor in the Israeli attitude. Another new element in the situation was the reported statement by the American owners of the *Observer* which was laying off Ismailia in Lake Timsah, that the ship needed to go into dry dock in Europe and so would have to be evacuated northwards.*

Further negotiations with both sides brought no solution to the problem, the Egyptians sticking to their position that, as they exercised sovereignty over the Canal, they alone could take the necessary steps to secure the evacuation of the ships, while the Israelis maintained that the agreement reached on 27 July meant that their consent was required before the ships could leave.

The Secretary-General did his best to be of assistance, but without result. When I saw Gohar on 21 January he presented me with a four-point proposal covering (1) Study of the problem; (2) Reconnaissance of the Canal; (3) Drawing up a plan for evacuation of the ships; (4) The evacuation operation itself. These proposals covered the whole Canal, not just the southern part. The intention was for a reconnaissance of the southern

* *Egyptian Gazette*, 31 January, 1968.

part to be carried out between 27 and 29 January, and this passed off without incident, our observers taking up their positions on both banks of the Canal. A reconnaissance of the northern part of the Canal—that is, from Ismailia to Port Said —was due to take place between 30 January and 2 February.

I flew to Cairo on 29 January and at 5.27 the next morning I telephoned to Gohar, informing him that I had been instructed by the Secretary-General to say that I was unable to give a guarantee that there would be no Israeli interference with the northwards reconnaissance. This message was the outcome of a meeting the Secretary-General had had the previous evening with Israel's permanent representative at the UN, who had expressed his great concern at the danger of serious military action if the northwards reconnaissance was carried out as planned. However, he said that he thought a solution of the problem was possible if rather more time was allowed for negotiations. I was therefore instructed to inform the Egyptian authorities of this immediately and to suggest a postponement of the reconnaissance to give time for further discussions. At 7.45 Gohar called me up to tell me that the Canal Authority's boats had already left Ismailia to begin their northerly reconnaissance. 'I am keeping my fingers crossed,' he added.

As one of the boats approached Talata Bridge at 7.53 am three warning shots were fired from the Israeli side, and the boat returned to Lake Timsah. At 9.50 the Egyptian liaison officer telephoned to the officer in charge of the UN operations centre at Ismailia to tell him that the reconnaissance would restart from Lake Timsah at 10.30. At 11.21 one of the Egyptian boats reached Talata Bridge and was greeted with fire from the Israeli side, a later inspection by our observers showing that it had apparently been hit by a 20mm bullet and by several rounds from 7mm automatic weapons. One member of the crew had been injured. Egyptian forces returned fire at 11.22, but firing stopped a minute later. These activities could only be observed by us from the west side of the Canal because the Israelis had refused our observers access to the east side.

At 11.28 Egyptian forces opened up with mortars and artillery close to the control centre at Ismailia and the Israelis returned the fire. A demand by us for a ceasefire to take effect at 12.30 pm was accepted by both sides, but it was three-quarters of an hour before the firing actually stopped.

Israeli opposition was effective in halting further work by the Egyptians for the evacuation of the trapped ships. The obstacles which we had come up against in the course of this affair show how difficult it is to reach a successful outcome in matters which cannot properly be considered controversial, even when agreement in principle has been reached between the parties concerned. Evacuation southwards would have enabled the Egyptians to find out the situation in that part of the Canal and so determine how long a proper clearance would take. Reconnaissance and evacuation northwards would have given them a complete picture of the Canal and of the work that required to be done in it. But once the ships had been evacuated the Egyptians would not be able to use the Canal Authority boats, which would have suited Israel's book. Possibly the presence of Russian ships in Port Said was one of the reasons why Israel opposed the idea of a northerly reconnaissance, though the main reason was presumably that the Israelis were determined not to be left out of the evacuation exercise. There is also inevitably some doubt as to how far the Egyptians were really interested in getting the ships out.

The ship-owners and insurance companies continued their efforts on behalf of the ships and their crews, and rather over a year later it looked as if a new attempt would be made to secure their release. But nothing came of it. When I came home for good in 1970 I was approached by some Norwegian ship-owners who had bought a French ship and its cargo lying in the Canal, and asked for my help in rescuing it. They had the idea of simply notifying both sides of a time when the ship proposed to sail and then sailing. This showed a fine spirit of adventure but I was bound to point out that any such scheme was doomed to fail. I said we would have to wait for a change in the political situation, and at that time I was hopeful that there might soon be one.

At the beginning of December, 1967, I paid a visit to our post on the east side of the Canal, driving from Hebron to Beersheba and then into Sinai, crossing the old armistice demarcation line near Um Qataf where the first clashes between Israelis and Egyptians had taken place on 5 June. Then we drove over the Mitla Pass where a great concentration of Egyptian men and machines had been destroyed by the Israelis from the air. Some miles from the Suez Canal I met the Israeli liaison officer, Lt-Colonel Ben Dov, and we were talking together when we heard the sound of firing. By the time we reached the Canal anti-aircraft guns had gone into action, and Ben Dov informed me that an Israeli plane had been shot down in the Gulf of Suez. We reported this to OP Blue, at the southern end of the Canal, with instructions that the message should be transmitted to the operations centre at El Kantara. But the message never reached the centre, because the observer failed to pass it on. For the first and only time an observer had to be removed for failure in his duty. (He had already been guilty of mistakes.) There had previously been occasional errors in reporting as, for example on 9 November when an observer on the Israeli side of the Canal reported that shots had been fired by an armoured car on the Egyptian side and that a jeep 200 metres south of his post had been hit and two Israeli soldiers wounded. This report went immediately via the El Kantara control centre to UNTSO Headquarters in Jerusalem and from there to the Secretary-General who sent it on to the Security Council. All this happened before we found that a mistake had been made. The Israeli liaison officer told us that the jeep had not been hit but had caught fire as the result of an explosion. It so happened that on this occasion the observer had been alone in his post, whereas we tried to ensure that all posts were normally manned all the time by two observers of different nationalities. We had to send out a correction which was embarrassing not only for us but also for the Secretary-General and the Security Council. But as time went on our reporting attained a very high standard.

There followed a relatively peaceful period on the Canal, but by contrast the first half of February, 1968, saw an intense exchange of fire in the Jordan Valley. As has been mentioned, we had no observers there, but all the same we managed, by invoking the Security Council resolution of June, 1967, to get the ceasefire restored on a number of occasions. The Secretary-General tried in vain to get the parties to agree to the establishment of an observer system. Part of the trouble was that Fateh let it be known that observers would be regarded as enemies.

During the winter the Israelis had announced that the annual military parade on their Independence Day (15 May) would be held in Jerusalem and would pass through the Arab sector of the city. This led to strong protests in the Arab countries and some Israeli newspapers expressed their opposition too. In April Jordan lodged an official protest, but the Israeli preparations went ahead, stands surrounded by barbed wire being erected capable of holding 60,000 people. Security precautions were strict, but the parade itself passed off without incident—and in spite of the fact that the Security Council had recommended that it should not be held.

Israel's attitude was unwise. If the object was to humiliate the Arabs still further, to rub into them the fact of their defeat and so to increase the hatred felt by them towards the conquerors, then the Israelis set about it in the right way. Indeed, it is hard to find any other explanation for their action. The parade had nothing to do with security. Perhaps its real purpose was to frighten as many Arabs into leaving Jerusalem as possible.

Unrest between Israel and Jordan continued. On 17 March there was a clash between guerrillas infiltrating from Jordan, who were backed by fire from Jordanian artillery, and Israeli forces. The following day a bus carrying schoolchildren was blown up by a mine north of Eilat. A doctor and a boy were killed and twenty-eight teachers and children injured. The Israelis claimed that between then and 15 February there had been thirty-five sabotage attacks mounted from Jordanian territory and strong warnings were given both by the Prime Minister, Levi Eshkol, and the Minister of Defence, Moshe Dayan. The expected Israeli reprisal took place on 21 March. Israeli forces crossed the River Jordan on a wide front between the Damia and Allenby Bridges, attacking guerrilla bases in the refugee camps. I called on both sides to observe the ceasefire but it was late in the afternoon before it could be re-established. When the operation had been completed the Israelis published a communiqué in which they asserted that all their objectives had been attained. Their losses had been estimated at twenty-one killed and ninety wounded and some equipment destroyed. At least 150 guerrilla soldiers were presumed to have been killed.

There was no doubt that the refugee camp at El-Karameh had been very badly hit. El-Karameh had been established by King Abdullah in an attempt to rescue the refugees from the miserable conditions in which they first had to exist after their flight in 1948. *Karameh* is the Arabic for 'dignity', and Abdullah's intention was that here the Arabs would be able to win back their dignity.

The guerrilla forces claimed a victory, maintaining that they had driven back the Israeli forces and captured some equipment. An Israeli tank and other weapons were put on show in Amman the following day when the funeral took place of those who had been killed in the fighting.

The Karameh incident was the subject of a debate in the Security Council, following a complaint by Jordan. Israeli military action was condemned and a general warning given to both parties. But fresh incidents in the Jordan valley continued, and again the Secretary-General asked for an observer system to be established, but again with no result. Jordan's refusal to agree to observers can only be regarded as extremely short-sighted. Not till towards the end of May, when it was harvest time in the valley, did conditions become more peaceful.

At the end of May I had a meeting in Cairo with Gohar at which I brought up the serious situation which had arisen for our observers. Egyptian positions had been creeping steadily nearer and nearer to some of our posts which thereby came in the direct line of fire whenever shooting broke out. We were demanding that there should be a gap of at least 50 metres between their military positions and our observation posts. There could have been no reasonable objection to this proposal as far as the Egyptians' defences were concerned, but we never managed to convince Gohar. On the East Bank conditions were somewhat better, because whereas the Egyptian defences were continuous the Israeli positions were fairly widely separated. Admittedly, once firing had started, Israeli armoured vehicles had a habit of placing themselves immediately behind our observation posts, thereby putting our observers in a direct line of fire, but by and large our problems on that side of the Canal were smaller.

In the middle of June, 1968, I went to UN Headquarters in New York for a nine-day visit to discuss our problems with U Thant and Bunche. The regular exchange of letters and telegrams needs to be supplemented from time to time by personal contact.

Before I left information came in that an Israeli patrol had been ambushed and wiped out on the Mediterranean coast east of Port Said. Though Egypt exercised full control over the Suez Canal for nine kilometres south of Port Said, there was an area inside Sinai where Egyptian and Israeli troops faced each other. We had no observers here, though after this and a couple of similar incidents we tried to get posts set up. But neither side was in favour.

At the beginning of July there was firing from the Egyptian side followed by Israeli reprisals against the town of Suez in which forty-seven people were killed and sixty-six injured. In the course of this incident there had been for the first time what was apparently a deliberate attack on one of our posts. It could not have been an accident that OP Red, on the East Bank of the Canal just north of Suez, had been subjected to small arms fire for half an hour, since the fire had originated from a point only 400m away, for the nearest Israeli position was 200m away, and the post was clearly marked with UN emblems. I went to Cairo to lodge a strong protest.

It was at about this time that an extremist group of Palestinian Arabs started to employ a new weapon—hijacking. An Israeli El Al plane was hijacked by the Popular Front for the Liberation of Palestine (PFLP) and compelled to land in Algeria. During the long—and eventually successful—negotiations for the plane's extradition, the Secretary-General and the Italian Government were among the many who found themselves involved. At the beginning of August the Israelis again used planes in an attack in the Jordan Valley which was aimed at destroying Fateh bases on the East Bank of the river.

When, inevitably, this incident came up for debate in the Security Council yet another attempt was made to get observers established in the area, but once again without success. There were also problems between Israel and Syria. When I met the new Syrian Chief of Staff, General M. Tlass, who had taken over from Sweidani in March, 1968, he brought up the question of the destruction by Israel of Arab villages in the occupied Golan area. Later we took this up with the Israelis, whose answer was that the defensive positions they were building in the area necessitated destruction of the villages.

Escalation along the Suez Canal continued. At the end of August we were told by Major Levinson, the Israeli Liaison Officer, that two Israeli jeeps had hit mines and two Israeli soldiers had been killed in an Egyptian ambush. A third soldier had been captured and taken back across the Canal. The Israelis demanded the immediate release of this soldier and made it clear that they regarded this not as an isolated incident but as the beginning of a new raiding policy by the Egyptians. I discussed the matter with Dayan in Tel Aviv and with Gohar in Cairo. Dayan insisted on a guarantee that there would be no repetition of the incident, 'otherwise we shall have to take whatever steps we feel necessary for the protection of our troops'. Gohar said he knew nothing about the affair. Israel complained to the Security Council, and instead of launching an immediate reprisal waited to see what would come out of the Security Council debate. But on 8 September trouble flared up again, heavy weapons being employed by both sides, and the result being the biggest exchange of fire since the sinking of the *Eilat*. Many civilians on the West Bank were killed and injured and now it was Egypt's turn to complain to the Security Council.

During this exchange several of our posts came under fire and were hit by artillery shells and mortar bombs. The Operations Centre at Ismailia was severely damaged, and later, with Egyptian agreement, we moved it 200m further back, keeping an observation post on the Canal bank. We sent strong protests to both sides.

Small Egyptian commando units now began regularly to cross the Canal for operations against the Israelis on the East

Bank. It was difficult for the Israelis to prevent this, for the Egyptians held every yard of their side, while the Israelis were much more thinly spread out. However, as one Israeli officer said one day, 'We can cross the Canal by helicopter and land wherever we like.' This is exactly what they were able to do later. These commando attacks naturally increased tension along the Canal, and on 26 October there was another intense exchange of fire. It appeared to have been the Egyptians who began it, but the Israelis made good use of the opportunity for a massive retaliation. On 4 November the Israeli Press announced that Israeli forces had carried out a commando raid by helicopter deep inside Egypt, destroying a power station and two bridges south of Luxor in Upper Egypt. The helicopters had presumably taken off from Sharm el-Shaikh, which had now become an important offensive Israeli base.

At the end of November there were several simultaneous explosions in Jerusalem, in which eleven people were killed and seventy injured. They were apparently caused by time-bombs planted in parked cars. In the space of a fortnight Palestinian guerrilla groups carried out a number of attacks on targets inside Israel, and on 1 and 2 December the Israelis struck back, sending a commando force deep into Jordan to destroy several bridges and cut road and rail communications between Amman and Aqaba, the country's only port. During a visit to Amman in November I discussed the situation with the Pakistani expert Sharfraz, who was in charge of the UN development programme in Jordan. He was very concerned about relations between the Government and Fateh, predicting that if there was no political solution a collision between them was inevitable. That prediction was to come true two years later.

While I was on leave at home over Christmas, Fateh attacked another Israeli plane, this time at Athens airport. There was extreme bitterness in Israel over this attack, and Lebanon was blamed for it because the guerrilla unit responsible had travelled to Athens in a Lebanese plane. So the following day Israeli troops landed by helicopter at Beirut civil airport and destroyed thirteen Arab planes on the ground. There was universal disapproval of this Israeli attack, and the

Security Council passed a strongly worded resolution condemning it. The Israelis insisted that their action was justified not simply by the Athens assault but also by a number of incidents which originated inside Lebanon. However, their reprisals had no effect on the guerrillas who continued to infiltrate over the border and carry out acts of sabotage and terror. The Lebanese authorities insisted that they did their best to step these activities but that there, as in Jordan, they were handicapped by the widespread sympathy felt for the Palestinians by the bulk of the population.

Before the June War the Chief of Staff of UNTSO was supposed to be responsible for plans to evacuate all UN personnel in the Middle East in the event of a crisis, but when war actually came it was shown that these plans were not easy to put into practice. A meeting in Beirut, at which representatives of all UN organizations in the Middle East were present, was called in which we worked out a new arrangement. This, which was approved by U Thant, laid it down that, while the Chief of Staff would continue to be responsible for planning and co-ordination, the actual execution of evacuation plans should be the responsibility of the organization which had the largest staff in each country. In practise this means that UNTSO now is responsible for putting evacuation into effect in Israel and in the occupied territories, while the UN Development Programme (UNDP) is similarly responsible in Egypt, Jordan and Syria, and the United Nations Works and Relief Agency (UNWRA) in Lebanon.

At the beginning of the New Year (1969) a new form of psychological warfare started up along the Canal. Troops on both sides of the Canal, which is only about 100m wide, started hurling abuse at each other. From our experience of this sort of thing in the Jerusalem area we knew how easily it could develop into a more lethal form of warfare, and we tried to warn both sides against letting it spread. Another variation which I noticed while carrying out an inspection of posts on the West Bank of the Canal was a large placard on the East Bank which read (in Arabic): 'Don't forget 1948, 1956, and 1967. Welcome to Israel. Remember Suez.'

The Egyptians used to snipe at Israeli troops using heavy

machinery to construct defensive positions (the Bar-Lev Line) along the East Bank. Bullets flew over the Canal and now and then struck our observation posts. We naturally protested most strongly, and also took steps to reinforce the shelters attached to the posts making them secure against direct hits by shells from 155mm guns and mortars. The officer in charge of the El Kantara Operations Centre, who was a coastal artillery expert, suggested that it might be better to keep our officers permanently in the shelters, letting them use periscopes for the purpose of observation. I did not feel able to agree to this proposal, since I felt it essential that we should maintain direct observation as far as that was possible. When I discussed the security problems with Gohar he always insisted that his hope was for some progress in negotiations towards a political solution, and there can be little doubt that this hope was shared by the majority of his countrymen.

Firing over the Canal went on, and mines continued to be laid on the East Bank by Egyptian commandos. This was comparatively easy for them in the area north of El Kantara where there was no proper metalled road. The outlook was not promising, but for a time the main focus of trouble shifted to other areas. On 18 February an Israeli plane was attacked at Zurich airport, one of the attackers being shot dead by a security guard on the plane. These tactics by the Palestinians did little harm to Israel; on the contrary, they tended to injure the Palestinians' case in the eyes of the world. As retaliations to guerrilla activity in the Israeli-occupied Golan area Israeli planes carried out a bombing attack on two Syrian villages, in which fifteen people were reported to have been killed. It was shortly after this that General Hafez el Asad seized power in Syria.

Mine explosions on the East Bank of the Canal continued and at the end of February the Israelis, who had not always directly answered Egyptian sniping or mining, began to increase their retaliation. One of the station wagons at OP Red was hit, and I was obliged to lodge a strong protest in Cairo. A great deal of my time was now being spent on tour along both sides of the Canal, and it was at this period (March, 1969) that the Egyptian Chief of Staff, General Abdel Munim Riad, was killed while observing an exchange of fire across the Canal. On one occasion when I had been invited for a meeting with the Egyptian Foreign Minister, Mahmoud Riad, he said to me: 'Is Egypt supposed to accept Israeli occupation of her territory, and if so for how long? Six months? Five years? Ninety-nine years? We have already seen part of our country occupied for two years. Are we supposed to just sit and watch while Israel colonises our own land? That is something we simply cannot accept.' This was in a sense the prologue to a new chapter, which was to bring a full-scale war of attrition along the Canal.

CHAPTER 11

A WAR OF ATTRITION

✤ ✤ ✤ ✤

Violations of the ceasefire now began to occur almost daily, and the conditions in which our observers had to carry out their duties became extremely onerous. They were obliged to spend many hours at a stretch in their shelters, and it was difficult to arrange for their relief. Often the vehicles taking them to or from their post would get caught in crossfire and they would have to jump out and seek what cover they could find. The periods they spent at their posts were increased to six and seven days, and sometimes as much as two weeks went by before we could arrange for their relief. In a letter of protest which I sent to both Dayan and Gohar I wrote that, while it was understandable that a post might be hit during a heavy exchange of fire, there had been many occasions recently when fire had been deliberately aimed at our posts and communications equipment. I sent a letter to the Secretary-General in the middle of March in which I tried to explain what was happening by saying that I thought the Egyptian aim (and at this time it was usually the Egyptians who started the firing) was presumably, by maintaining intense activity along the Canal, to draw attention to the seriousness of the situation, to boost morale in the army, and to demonstrate the effectiveness of the new weapons that had been obtained from the Soviet Union. They also naturally hoped to interrupt the construction of Israeli fortifications on the East Bank.

I travelled continuously between Jerusalem and Cairo as well as carrying out my inspection on both banks of the Canal. As I have explained, it was impossible for me to make a direct crossing of the Canal, so that if, for example, I had been on the East Bank and wanted to get to the other side, I had to go back to Jerusalem, fly to Cairo, and then drive to the West Bank—an extremely clumsy and time-consuming arrangement.

We moved our Operations Centre on the East Bank 50km back from El Kantara to Rafah on the road to Gaza. One observation post which was destroyed had also to be moved, which created fresh communications problems. OP Juliet was one of those which suffered most because an Egyptian position had been constructed round it. There was, as has been mentioned, a tendency for the Egyptians to come closer and closer to our posts, but in spite of the extremely difficult working conditions our observers' reports became more rather than less exact. At the end of March U Thant asked me whether I would consider extending my term as Chief of Staff. 'I regard it as very important,' he said in his letter, 'that you should continue as Chief of Staff after May 1969. Your experience and knowledge of the situation, as well as your good relations with the parties, would be very difficult, if not impossible, to replace. I therefore take pleasure in offering you an extension for a further period of two years until 16 May, 1971. I very much hope that you will find it possible to accept this proposed extension.' This letter showed an appreciation of my work which I naturally welcomed, and advanced strong arguments which I could not lightly dismiss. My answer was that I could not, with regret, agree to two more years but that I was prepared to accept an extension till 1 December, 1969. As things turned out the date of my retirement was to be postponed again, first to 1 May and then to 31 July, 1970.

Difficulties in the way of keeping in touch with the posts increased. The report of one radio operator covering the week 8–16 April shows that he set out on the morning of the 10th towards the posts on the east side of the Canal, only to run into fire as he approached OP Silver which obliged him to take cover in the desert until nightfall, when he returned to the Operations Centre. The next day he spent two hours in the shelter of OP Pink and returned to the Operations Centre a long time after dark. On 12 April he managed to reach OP Yellow without incident. On 13 April he was again caught on his way to OP Pink, taking cover in the desert for two hours. The same thing happened to him the next day on his way from OP Red to OP Blue, taking cover for an hour and a half, and when he reached OP Blue sitting in the shelter there for a long time. On the 15th he again spent half the day in the shelter of OP Blue which was under heavy artillery fire, and when on the 16th he managed to leave the post he was again caught in crossfire and obliged to take cover in the desert. It is obvious that these conditions imposed a great strain on the officers involved; it also considerably slowed up their work. Here was an officer spending six days on a task which would normally have been completed in two.

The Secretary-General did what he could to help us. He prepared a letter to be sent to both sides, and when we saw the draft we suggested stiffening the passages in it that referred to the safety of the UN Staff. One of the points on which we were particularly insistent was the need for a space 50m on each side of our posts, and 500m behind them, in which all military positions should be forbidden. The Secretary-General's letter was sent to the Security Council on 21 April and the Press interpreted its language as meaning that he was considering withdrawing the observation posts. But at that time this was not a realistic proposition and was officially denied. In his letter the Secretary-General stated that the ceasefire had broken down, and he concluded with unqualified praise for the observers and for the work which they were doing.

On 22 April the Irish Major Joseph Young was wounded when his car drove over a mine on the way to OP Green—the most northerly post on the East Bank—where he was on duty. The car was completely wrecked, and it was a miracle that he was not killed. The first reports had been that he was seriously wounded, but even so it took 7½ hours before we could get him into hospital. It was then found that his injuries were not as serious as we had feared, but this shows the sort of nightmare conditions in which we had to operate, right up to the time when my service ended.

This incident demonstrated how impotent we were when it was a question of getting our own people evacuated. We had our own ambulance at El Kantara with Red Cross markings,

163

but as soon as it set off to collect Major Young it came under fire. It was only when dark fell that we were able to pick him up with the aid of a helicopter which the Israelis had put at our disposal. The affair made a deep impression on the observers, who found themselves in the middle of an active war where they were shot at by both sides—and later also attacked from the air. Their attitude was: 'We came here to observe and report on an armistice; now we are reporting on a war. Isn't it time that we received a new mandate from the Security Council?' This was perfectly understandable, but it was not easy to satisfy them. Bunche thought it would be unwise to expect the Security Council to give us a new mandate at a time when the big powers were in open disagreement.

The Commander of UN forces in Kashmir, the Canadian General Bruce McDonald, once said in a lecture: 'Believe me, it is neither easy nor pleasant to be part of a UN force; however, it is a good deal easier and pleasanter than fighting a war.' Hitherto I would have fully subscribed to this statement, but after the war of attrition started along the Canal in March, 1969, when the observers were obliged to take punishment from both sides without being able to defend themselves in any way, it became harder to maintain morale than it is in a real war. Yet, remarkably enough, morale did remain at a high level.

Our biggest headache was OP Green, which became increasingly difficult of access owing to Egyptian mine-laying and shooting on the road leading to it. Many times the suggestion was made that we should close the post down, but as it was one of our most important posts we were reluctant to take this step. The Israeli army made great use of tracked vehicles, and every morning the dirt road was carefully checked for mines before Israeli lorries were sent along it. We used to protect ourselves as best we could by driving a few hundred yards behind the Israeli vehicles, but of course this was no protection against Egyptian fire. One day, when a group of observers had been ordered to proceed after an Israeli convoy, one of the officers refused. This was the only breach of discipline on the Canal front during all my time as head of UNTSO. The officer involved was sent home and a replacement for him provided. It was at about this time that we raised the question of supplying the observers with armoured vehicles.

After Israeli commandos had carried out a new attack against bridges and power lines in Upper Egypt on 1 May we had two rather more peaceful months on the Canal. I paid a short visit to UN Headquarters in New York for consultation in June and then had two weeks' holiday in Norway. While I was in New York I gave my first and only Press Conference as Head of UNTSO, and I think it went well. On the whole my relations with the Press were good and I found journalists of all nationalities with whom I had to deal understanding. I was fortunate in having a very experienced Press Officer, Grand, who had been present at the Rhodes armistice negotiations in 1949. We were, of course, often criticized in the Press, parti- cularly in the Israeli Press, but there was usually nothing we could do about it unless a completely baseless story appeared. Then we would make a complaint through the Israeli Foreign Ministry. On one occasion the Foreign Ministry actually issued a correction.

By the time I returned to Jerusalem the situation had greatly deteriorated. For the first time since the June War fighter aircraft had in July been involved in the Canal fighting, the Israelis making particular use of them. The danger to our observers increased, especially to those on the West Bank who were exposed to Israeli air attacks on Egyptian targets close to their posts. In the course of a report to the Security Council on 7 July U Thant said: 'Even though the UN military obser- vers in the Canal sector carry out their duties in a praiseworthy manner, they are now exposed to constant danger.' He referred to the fact that numerous protests by UNTSO had not been heeded, and that in June alone the Egyptian forces had fired twenty-one times on UN personnel or positions and Israeli forces five times. 'I must warn the Security Council,' he added, 'that if firing against UN observers continues a point will be reached when I shall have no other choice but to advise the Security Council to withdraw the observers.' However, we were to continue as we were for another year after the Secretary-General's emphatic warning. By then, fortunately, what had seemed to be a certain preliminary to another war came to a stop. But much was to happen in that year.

Only a few days after the Secretary-General's report the Egyptians sent a commando raid of eight rubber boats, with six to eight men in each boat, across the southern part of the Canal. The Israelis were taken by surprise; three soldiers were killed and an armoured car destroyed. The observers at OP Mike saw what was going on but did not report it because, as the Secretary-General had said in his report, they regarded the ceasefire as having completely broken down. Also, had they reported it, they would have been obliged to mention what could be regarded as intelligence material of the sort that should not be transmitted over the radio *en clair*.

The situation was a delicate one. It was obvious that the Egyptians had broken the agreement of 27 July, 1967, respecting the use of the Canal. So a directive was sent out to the effect that in future all such violations should be reported, and the next time I saw Gohar I told him of this.

Israel retaliated with a number of air strikes, particularly against targets on the West Bank of the Canal, including the Sweet Water Canal which runs parallel to the Suez Canal and provides Port Said with its water. This was badly damaged. 19 and 20 July saw the most intensive exchanges since the June War, with air battles in which there were losses on both sides. I had meetings in Jerusalem and Cairo which achieved nothing. We had serious discussions among ourselves whether or not we should close down our observation posts and only leave the operations headquarters on both sides of the Canal which could be used as a nucleus for reactivating the posts should the situation improve. But we decided to carry on. I felt that as UNTSO was the only body capable of observing and reporting objectively from the Canal area we should stick it out as long as was physically possible. My attitude was strengthened by the fact that, at a meeting which their delegates had with U Thant, none of the Governments with observers in the field called for their withdrawal.

However, the debate was inevitably renewed after the Swedish Major Roland Plane had been killed on 15 July by Israeli artillery fire at OP Mike in Port Tewfiq. He was a very fine officer. A protest was sent to the Israeli authorities, and when after ten days' continuous fighting the air attacks ceased the situation improved somewhat. All the same, we had from time to time to order the temporary closure of some of the posts because it simply became much too dangerous to go on manning them. For a long time we had only five posts operational on each side of the Canal instead of the usual nine. During the period from 1 June, 1969, to 12 February, 1970, our observation posts were fired on 345 times, 284 times from the Egyptian side and 61 from the Israeli side. The Operations Centre at Ismailia was in the line of fire practically every day.

Firing and commando attacks across the Canal continued throughout the autumn of 1969. The firing varied in intensity and many hits were registered close to our posts. Israeli reprisals for Egyptian commando raids were now directed not so much against Egyptian positions on the West Bank, which were well defended, as on targets deep inside Egypt.

It was a miracle that more observers were not killed. On 10 September I had a meeting in Cairo with General Fawzi, the Egyptian Minister of War, at which I took up the question of measures for the protection of the observers. The preliminary need was to get the ceasefire restored, but it was also essential that the observation posts should not be fired at, that their shelters should be strengthened, a security zone around them established, and assistance given for the evacuation of wounded. I discussed the same points with the Israelis, but there was little change in the overall situation except that the shelters were strengthened.

At the end of October we had to face another difficult problem which could have brought our operations on the Suez Canal to a halt. All our posts were well marked, the vehicles and caravans being painted white with the letters UN on them in black and the UN flag flying from their radio antennae. In addition there was a large square panel painted white with the letters UN in black on it which was illuminated at night so that everybody could see where the UN positions were. Egypt now claimed that these lights could be used by Israeli planes as navigational aids and demanded their removal. As the Canal was a little more than 100m wide the Israelis had many better navigational aids than these lights and we refused to extinguish them, whereupon the Egyptians said they would take their own steps to get rid of them. I told Gohar that it was absolutely essential, from the point of view of the observers' safety, that the lights should remain. He suggested that we should only man the posts in daylight, but this would have been impossible because of the difficulty of transporting officers to and from the posts. Eventually a compromise was reached after we had screened the lights from above so that they were made invisible from the air.

Although the bulk of our work was now concentrated in the Canal area I tried to continue my visits to the other fronts as often as possible. The situation on the Syrian front was a good deal quieter, in spite of several Syrian acts of sabotage and Israeli reprisals. Gradually the Israeli positions along the ceasefire line had encroached too near our observation posts, but when the Israelis claimed that they wanted the ground we were on for military purposes we agreed to move. We had, as has been said, no observation posts either on the Jordanian or the Lebanese front, so that we could do nothing about the guerrilla activities mounted in both these countries, whose Governments constantly proclaimed their wish to maintain the ceasefire.

When the Aqsa Mosque at Jerusalem, one of the most venerable shrines of the Islamic world, was set on fire on 21 August, 1969, there was a great outcry in all the Arab countries and they called for the setting up of an International Commission to investigate the origins of the fire. Israel would not agree, and set up its own commission of enquiry. The man responsible for the outrage turned out to be a deranged Australian, who was tried and imprisoned. The Israeli Prime Minister, Golda Meir, offered to contribute towards the repair of the mosque but this was declined by the Moslem authorities.

The American-owned oil pipeline (TAP-line), which links the oilfields of Saudi Arabia with the sea terminal in Lebanon, was blown up by Palestinian guerrillas in May, and the oil did not start flowing along it again until September. This action, which damaged the Arab countries as much as—or more than—the Americans, was the sort of thing which did the Palestinian cause no good.

These were just two of the incidents which contributed to the increasing tension in the Middle East during the summer of 1969 and made me decide to defer my retirement into the New Year. I was still hoping to see a political settlement before I finally left.

At Christmas came the Israeli coup whereby five gunboats, which had been ordered by Israel but impounded by the French authorities when the delivery of arms to both sides was forbidden at the time of the June War, were smuggled out of France by Israeli agents helped by a Norwegian. This was gunboat diplomacy with a vengeance.

After much discussion in the UN Secretariat and with the various Middle East Governments we were finally authorized to acquire two Saracen-type AVs to be used for the transport of UN personnel in the Canal area. The vehicles came from British forces in Cyprus, and were to begin with stationed on the East Bank and manned by Finnish troops.

Just before Christmas the United States took the initiative in an effort to get the ceasefire restored both along the Suez Canal and in the Jordan Valley. The American administration had become increasingly concerned about the situation in the Middle East, and particularly deplored Israeli deep penetration raids on Egypt, one of which had just killed eighty people in a factory near Cairo. In Jordan differences between King Hussein and the guerrillas seemed to be coming to a head, and though for a moment these were patched over the atmosphere inside the country continued extremely tense.

On 14 February I flew to New York to discuss the situation with U Thant and Bunche. Bunche, who met me at the airport, told me he thought that if the Security Council Resolution of November, 1967, (242) had been tabled now it would not have passed, so far had the attitudes of the big powers diverged. I put forward three alternative proposals for the future of our observer organization on the Canal: All the posts to be withdrawn and only the control centres kept; a partial withdrawal, leaving three posts on either side of the Canal; pull the posts back from the Canal bank further inland. The Secretary-General preferred the third alternative, but when I took it up with the Israeli and Egyptian authorities I found them not in favour of it. So we continued as we were, though with rather fewer posts manned. I also discussed the question of my successor with the Secretary-General. I told him that 31 July was absolutely the latest date for my departure, and recommended Colonel Siilasvuo as my successor. He had now been two years with UNTSO and had done excellent work.

Throughout February and March the observation posts along the Canal were fired on almost every day. The observers did a fantastic job, and in an interview with a New York paper Bunche referred to them as 'the Middle East's unknown heroes'. He said that, thanks to them, the war along the Canal was 'the best reported war in history'. These are the names of the officers in charge of the Operation Centres:

El Kantara Operations Centre
   Major Roy E. Skinner, Australian Army
   Major Charles Gautier, French Army
   Lieutenant-Colonel Sein Tun, Burmese Army
   Lieutenant-Colonel Dick A. Lago-Lengquist, Swedish Army
   Lieutenant-Colonel Keith D. Howard, Australian Army
   Lieutenant-Colonel Jens E. Bögvad, Swedish Army
   Major Norbert F. Mandl, Austrian Army

Ismailia Operations Centre
   Lieutenant-Colonel Carl O. Rosenius, Swedish Army
   Major Olov K. Ljungkvist, Swedish Air Force
   Major Henri P. Duhem, French Army
   Lieutenant-Colonel Pearse T. P. Quinlan, Irish Army

All deserve the highest commendation for the services they performed, which made it possible for the UN operations along the Canal to be successfully carried out even after the war of attrition started in March, 1969.

On 31 March we received notice from the Egyptian authorities that no aircraft would be allowed to overfly the Delta area, the reason presumably being that by now an air defence system of SAM-2s and SAM-3s had been installed round Cairo and Alexandria. This meant that for us the distance between Jerusalem and Cairo was more than doubled and the Dakota which we had been using on this run was no longer suitable. The Swiss Government came to our rescue by placing at our disposal via the Bell Air Company a ten-seater Falcon 20 jet, most of the expense of which they generously footed.

Around this time there were several Egyptian ambushes along the Canal, to which the Israelis replied with attacks on Egyptian positions by artillery and from the air. It was now, also, that we first learned that Israel had been equipped with American Phantom fighter-bombers.

Unrest spread to the Lebanon, with clashes between Palestinian guerrillas and armed Lebanese, with the army trying on the whole to keep out. The situation in the country was extremely unstable, but the authorities stuck to their determination not to allow the guerrillas to operate from bases inside Lebanon. The Lebanese, in fact, were now facing the same problem that had for so long confronted Jordan, and here too the official ruling was not always obeyed owing to the sympathy for the guerrillas felt by large sections of the population. But eventually a compromise agreement was patched up.

By now my tour of duty was drawing to a close. I had arranged with the Secretary-General that I should take two months of the leave due to me from the end of April, and accordingly we drove up through Syria and Turkey and then by air across Europe to Oslo. This time my luck held: no summons brought me prematurely back to duty, and Siilasvuo successfully held the fort on my behalf. While I was away the cycle of guerrilla attacks and air reprisals continued, and just after I returned the Swedish Lt-Colonel Jens E. Bögvad was killed near OP Blue by machine-gun fire from the Egyptian side of the Canal while he and other officers were reconnoitring a new site for the post. Another officer was slightly wounded. I sent a strong protest to Cairo and received in reply a note deploring the incident and stating that a commission of enquiry was being set up to discover who had been responsible for it. In Bögvad the UN lost an unusually fine and able officer.

A round of farewells followed—in Egypt, Israel, Jordan, Lebanon and Syria. There were many old friends to say good-bye to, and it would be invidious to try to measure the degree of friendship which my wife and I met everywhere. In the course of my narrative I may not have given any general picture of the Arab officials with whom I had to deal, and whom we were now visiting for the last time, but this is not because I found them less than capable and intelligent men. They may sometimes lack the diplomatic and political dynamism of their Israeli counterparts, but they are just as wise.

It was with some feeling of satisfaction that I contemplated my last days in Jerusalem. The ceasefire for which we had worked so hard had been approved by both parties. The initiative of the American Secretary of State, William Rogers, had been accepted by Egypt and a ceasefire along the Canal was to come into force at the beginning of August. Admittedly the main objective—a political solution—seemed as far off as ever. When making my farewells to Golda Meir she said to me: 'If we do get a peace settlement I shall ask my Government to invite you to be present when the peace treaty is signed.' I look forward to that day.

On 31 July, my last day in Government House, I received a letter from U Thant and a telegram of greetings from Ralph Bunche. U Thant's letter is reproduced on page 198. Bunche's telegram read: 'On this your last day as Chief of Staff of UNTSO, I want to extend to you my personal good wishes and express to you my appreciation of all that you have done in your 7 years as Chief of Staff.

'We have worked together closely for the whole of this period in all sorts of situations and conditions, and I can appreciate better than most the challenges you have had to face and your quiet and firm way of dealing with them. The job of Chief of Staff of UNTSO is, even in the best of circumstances, a difficult and complex one, poised as it is between the parties of the Middle East conflict. I think that the United Nations has been lucky to have had as its Chief of Staff in the Middle East in these very difficult years a professional officer of high standing who has at the same time managed to maintain the United Nations position in the face of all sorts of pressures and to remain on excellent terms with all of the parties to the conflict and their various Military and Civilian Authorities. May I say that I personally have enjoyed our association and I hope that we shall have a chance from time to time to renew our personal friendship. I wish you and Mrs Bull all the very best in the years to come.'

Hardly less gratifying for someone who had striven always to maintain the spirit of impartiality which the post demanded but which critics were by no means always willing to concede was the leading article which appeared in the main English-language daily of Israel, the *Jerusalem Post*. Under the heading 'Bull Goes' this read: 'The relations between Israel and the United Nations Truce Supervision Organization have not always been wholly cordial. In fact, there were periods when the behaviour and obvious bias of some of the Chiefs of Staff of UNTSO caused resentment here and the critical view of their attitude proved later to be fully justified. One need only recall Generals Bennike of Denmark and Von Horn of Sweden, both of whom confirmed everybody's worst suspicions in the written accounts of their service here. The Canadian General Burns was more fair, but he too, was not always a model of impartiality.

'Of the many Chiefs of Staff of UNTSO, two will be remembered here with regard and affection. The first was General Riley, who served in the early 'fifties and won much respect for the manner in which he handled his assignment. Last week Israel bid farewell to General Odd Bull, who completed a term of duty which stretched over seven years, a long period which included the Six Day War and its aftermath.

'General Bull has earned our respect for his integrity, honesty and objectivity. A calm personality, the former Commander of the Norwegian Air Force came here in a period of relative tranquillity. He followed General Von Horn, who was not endowed with the same attributes, and was able very quickly to re-establish confidence and develop effective working relations with the Israel Army and Foreign Ministry. Unlike his immediate predecessor, he was not given to impatient outbursts and intemperate accusations. He consistently stayed out of the limelight, refusing press and television interviews. He remained at his post even when his headquarters was occupied by the Jordanian forces in the morning hours of the fateful June 5, 1967. Late that afternoon Israeli troops were able to free him and his associates and take them to safety in the Jewish section then under shelling.

'The General was also faithful in carrying out missions entrusted him by the Israeli Government. It was he who conveyed to Hussein Mr Eshkol's plea to keep out of the war, a plea that was foolishly spurned by the King, whose territory would have remained intact had he not done Nasser's bidding. Later General Bull was instrumental in arranging the ceasefire details with the Syrians and Egyptians and made attempts to supervise them. His good offices were made use of to arrange the exchange of prisoners and he helped in many other delicate matters.

'The Arab States could not muster the same enthusiasm for General Bull as for some of his predecessors, but despite Israel's appreciation of his work they were never heard to object to any of his efforts or to complain of his attitude.

'After the Six Day War, when the prestige of the United Nations, its Secretary-General, its entire Truce Supervision Organization and especially the manner in which the Emergency Force was withdrawn from Gaza and Sinai, plunged low, Israelis never lost their respect for General Bull. When the pressure of events allowed, it was also noticed that he had wide non-military interests, which ranged from music and art to literature. He was a frequent visitor to Art Galleries and an attentive listener to the Philharmonic.

'Israel regrets having to bid goodbye to this untypical representative of the United Nations. He worked hard for peace. Now that a glimmer of peace looms on the horizon, the job has fallen to the Finnish General Siilasvuo who will be shouldering a major post if and when the ceasefire takes effect. One would wish that the successor of General Bull should follow in his footsteps, which is a sufficient tribute to the retiring, quiet Norwegian. Israelis wish General Bull a much earned rest and to know that he will be remembered with appreciation and gratitude.'

Before I finally left Jerusalem on 1 August I paid a visit to the Hadassah Hospital where Jim Lang, a fine man who had for years rendered yeoman service to the UN and was No. 2 on my administration staff, lay ill with an incurable disease. On my way back I paused for a moment at the spot where Count Bernadotte had been assassinated in 1948.

CHAPTER 12

SOME LESSONS

✽ ✽ ✽ ✽

More than seven years spent as a servant of the United Nations in the Middle East have led me to formulate some general principles which I think should be adopted in any similar peace-keeping operation.

1. The head of any peace-keeping organization must be genuinely neutral and not simply objective. Privately he may make his own opinions known and may give advice, but in all negotiations he must observe the strictest neutrality. I am sure that it was only by the rigid observance of this rule that I was able to retain the confidence of all parties until the completion of my mission. To be successful the head of such an organization must be able to count on the services of efficient and experienced political and legal advisers.

2. Where the effective supervision of demilitarized zones is required, this can only be done if military forces are stationed on the ground. The experience of UNTSO showed that observers alone are not enough.

3. Demarcation lines, and any boundaries which are to be the object of international supervision, must be clearly marked out on the ground. This had been done in Kashmir (India–Pakistan conflict). There an 800km ceasefire line in very difficult mountain terrain was marked by UN observers with the co-operation of the parties.

4. If experts are brought in to clarify any aspect of the operation these must be supplied by the UN itself. There must be no reliance on experts supplied by any of the interested parties.

5. International servants must always remember that none of the problems with which they will be called upon to deal are

going to be wholly black or wholly white. Everything will be some shade of grey. (In my own experience I would make only one exception to this rule, and that is the situation of the Palestinian refugees. This is wholly black.)

6. International servants must bear in mind that all the parties with which they are involved will try to use the UN for their own purposes, and they will have to resist this pressure. I should record that I did not feel personally subjected to such pressure to any great extent, though I know that many of my subordinates were very conscious of it.

7. Observers must be selected with great care by the countries which have undertaken to provide them. It is in everybody's interest that only the best should be chosen. They should be between 25 and 40 years old and in first-class health. (Fitness may not have been so important before the June War of 1967, but during the period of war of attrition along the Canal in 1969 and 1970 it was the younger and fitter officers who came out the best.) Observers must be capable of putting up with isolation, a hostile environment, climatic extremes, and unjustified criticism. They ought not to serve for longer than a year unless they are selected to fill key positions. Officers who have responsibility for troops (those with UNEF, for example) can obviously be expected to serve longer.

8. Special operations which carry with them, as it were, the seal of a UN guarantee (as, for example, the Mount Scopus convoy) should only be undertaken if equipped with UN personnel and vehicles. All loading and unloading should be carried out under UN control.

9. There should be equal pay for equal work. This has not hitherto been the rule in UN operations, where each contingent has been paid according to its national scale. We saw this contrast particularly sharply in Gaza, where the pay of the Indian troops was very low, whereas troops from South American and Scandinavian countries received a special allowance. There is always the danger that poorly paid troops will be susceptible to the temptation to make money by reselling goods available to them at privileged rates, or to more serious abuses of their position.

10. The UN has to pay very varying rates for the services of

177

different national contingents. Scandinavian countries make a high charge—and this is no doubt one of the reasons why Norway was not asked to contribute forces to the Cyprus peace-keeping operation.

11. Co-operation between forces from countries of the most widely different political and cultural traditions is perfectly possible when there is a practical job to be done.* One of the pleasantest memories of my years of service in the Middle East is of the daily co-operation between people of all nationalities. In UNTSO we had representatives of 35 countries on the civilian side, all of whom had been recruited by the UN Secretariat in New York,† and 17 countries provided officers for the observer corps. Of course problems cropped up from time to time, but they were usually of a fairly trivial nature and never damaged overall co-operation. Our experience was a lesson in miniature of how international co-operation can succeed.

12. We have seen how much easier it is for the Security Council or General Assembly to pass a resolution embodying a principle than to get this principle implemented in the field. Examples of this were the setting up of UNEF in 1956, setting up of the observer system along the Suez Canal in 1967, and, last but not least, the Security Council resolution of 22 November, 1967, which has still to be implemented.

❊   ❊   ❊

What of the future? In his report to the UN General Assembly on 27 June, 1948, Folke Bernadotte recommended that all refugees should have an opportunity to return home and to

* It is true that there were no contingents or observers from Communist countries either in Lebanon or in UNTSO, except for the Yugoslav contingent in UNEF. At one stage I was offered personnel from East European countries and said that I would welcome them, but for some reason they never arrived. It is true that the Soviet Union (like France) refused to contribute to the special peace-keeping budget of the United Nations, which paid for UNEF but it was a contributor to the ordinary budget, which covered the expenses of UNTSO. Bunche's attitude was to wait until a Communist government pressed him to accept personnel from it; but, strange to say, this pressure never came.

† Locally recruited personnel brought the total up to 40.

recover the property which they had lost. The plight of the refugees was something which he felt very acutely, since he had probably had more direct experience of this tragic problem than anybody else. In his final report, dated 16 September, 1948 (the day before he was murdered), he again emphasized that the return of the refugees must be given top priority if many thousands of them were to be saved from death.

On 11 December, 1948, the General Assembly passed a resolution recommending that all refugees who wished to return to their homes and who were prepared to live at peace with their neighbours should have the opportunity to do so as soon as was practically possible. Those who did not wish to return, the resolution continued, should receive compensation for the property which they had lost according to the principles laid down by international law and by equity. As has already been mentioned, it was only to be a tiny fraction of the refugees which was in fact able to return home. The rest remained in exile and constitute the most considerable problem which the world faces in the Middle East.

This 1948 resolution has been confirmed yearly at every subsequent session of the UN. Israel has refused to allow repatriation of the Arab population, allegedly on grounds of security, claiming this would mean the creation of a large permanent fifth column which could destroy the new state, though it is worth recalling that in November, 1947 (before the establishment of the State of Israel), the Zionists were prepared to accept the UN partition plan which would have created a Jewish state in which almost half the population would have been Arab. It is also significant that the property which the Arabs had left behind them was of great assistance in settling the flood of new Jewish immigrants. The UN estimated in 1951/2 that this Arab property was worth £100m.

Israel declared its willingness to absorb the refugees in the Gaza Strip, provided it was granted sovereignty over the area. This was of course a bit of political bargaining. The Israelis often claim that the refugees are used by the Arab Governments as pawns, without consideration for their real welfare, which would be best looked after if they were settled in some of the vast empty spaces to be found in the Arab world. There is an element of truth in this, but the most important fact is that from the start the Palestinians themselves have refused to abandon any of the rights which they insist they still hold in Palestine. After they had tenaciously maintained this attitude for some years it became impossible for any Arab Government or Arab leader to advocate policies running counter to their wishes. It is possible to say that the problem of the refugee became 'Palestinized'.

Many educated Palestinians gradually settled down in other Arab countries and took up employment there. They were able to give a good account of themselves, thanks to their efficiency and industry. But even these lucky ones for the most part refused to give up what they regarded as their right eventually to return to their home. And they saw this right recognized year after year by the General Assembly.

It is important in this respect to emphasize the fact that the Arab countries do not constitute a single nation, but a culture which is held together largely by religion and language. This majority culture has in the past shown itself extremely tolerant towards Christian and Jewish minorities. In Egypt the Copts, who are the descendants of the people who were there when the invading Arab armies came in the 7th century, constitute about ten per cent of the population. In Iraq can be found descendants of Babylonians, Assyrians and other former dominant peoples, all of whom have become to a large extent arabized. In Palestine were to be found descendants of Canaanites and Philistines, as well as of the Jews, who also had become arabized.

After the armistice agreements had been signed in 1949 various plans were drawn up for providing the refugees with new homes. Possible sites in Northern Syria and Iraq were investigated, but the Palestinians themselves showed not the slightest willingness to move.

As a Norwegian I can appreciate that in theory the Germans could, in the Second World War, have decided that Jutland was so strategically important to them that it must be incorporated in Germany and its inhabitants compelled to leave and resettle in Norway, where a language similar to their own is spoken. But this would hardly have been acceptable to either

Norway or Denmark. The Palestinians, if they had been forcibly removed to Iraq, would have felt much the same as the Jutlanders. They would have found themselves a minority among neighbours who in many respects were very dissimilar to them. (A majority of Iraqis are Shia Moslems whereas almost all Palestinian Arabs are Sunni Moslems or Christians.) Besides, most of the refugees were peasants, and the surrounding Arab countries already had a surplus of them. If the newcomers had been given priority in respect of land and capital (and how else could they have been resettled?) this would inevitably have aroused jealousy and bitterness in those among whom they were to live. One would be tempted to suspect that the only explanation for such a population transfer would be if it formed part of the divide and rule policy which outside powers have so often and so effectively pursued in the Middle East.

Israel's fear about the possible effect of having to receive hundreds of thousands of refugees is understandable. But what the refugees were in fact demanding was, in the first instance, only to be able to exercise a choice. How many would, when it came to the point, have opted for repatriation, it is impossible to say. A majority of expert opinion is that not more than ten per cent would choose to go back if this entailed living under alien rule. This was borne out by an investigation made on behalf of the US Senate's Foreign Relations Committee in 1960. It would have been quite possible for Israel to have absorbed this quantity of refugees and so remove the greatest obstacle towards a peaceful settlement. But the gesture was not made, and so the refugee problem has grown like a cancerous tumour which will now have to be excised before there can be any prospect of peace and understanding between Israel and her neighbours.

When in 1967 the Israeli armies occupied the remainder of Palestine, including the Gaza Strip, and in addition Sinai and the Golan Heights, an entirely new refugee problem was created and in addition the old problem was made a great deal worse. In August 1967 the Secretary-General of the UN reported that over 100,000 from the post-1948 refugee camps and 200,000 other Arabs had been rendered homeless as a result of the war. A great majority of those who had been in camps on the West Bank, round Jericho, Nablus and Hebron, had fled for a second time and were now squatting on the East Bank. This fresh exodus created huge problems.

Determined efforts were made to secure the repatriation of those who had fled from the Jordan Valley, but of those who signified their wish to return (estimated to be as high as 60 per cent), and filled in the necessary papers, only ten per cent managed to make it. None of those who came from the refugee camps in the valley were allowed back. The camps there stood empty, while their former inhabitants suffered terrible hardships in tents and other temporary accommodation on the bleak hills of the East Bank during the first winter of 1967/8.

The stream of refugees did not stop when the war stopped. For many months afterwards a steady trickle made its way eastwards across the River Jordan, including quite large numbers from the Gaza Strip. The Israelis encouraged their departure by various means, just as they had in 1948. Eventually the Jordanian authorities clamped down and closed the border.

* * *

A vital part of the Security Council's Resolution 242 is that which mentions the need to find a just solution of the refugee problem as the prerequisite for a durable political solution. Experts believe that most of the Palestinian refugees in camps could be resettled on both banks of the Jordan Valley, that new land could be brought under cultivation and new light industry started, if full use was made of the water and other resources available. The great advantage of resettlement here is that it would be inside—or only just outside—the borders of Palestine. The remaining refugees could probably be settled in the Gaza Strip, in Sinai (once the Israelis have fulfilled their obligation to withdraw), and in neighbouring Arab States.

The potentialities of the Jordan Valley were first demonstrated by the enterprise of a remarkable Palestinian, Musa Alami, whom I came to know well during my time in Jerusalem. He belonged to one of the oldest Arab families in Jerusalem, had been educated at Cambridge and was called to the English Bar. Returning to Palestine he joined the mandatory administration, becoming Government Advocate and Adviser on Arab affairs to the High Commissioner, but threw up Government service in 1937 when the Palestine Arabs were in open revolt against the British Government and its policy of greatly increased Jewish immigration. In 1945 the Arab League set up, at Musa's prompting, an Arab Development Society which was aimed at improving the economic position of the Palestinian peasants and teaching them new skills. After the catastrophe of 1948 Musa Alami determined to use the remaining funds of the ADS on behalf of the refugees. Against all expert advice he was convinced that water was to be found beneath the arid sun-baked desert of the valley—one of the hottest places in the world. At first with picks and shovels, and then with a primitive drill, Musa Alami and a few refugee helpers started digging. After five months their efforts were rewarded. Sweet water was found, and an experimental farm started. Gradually this grew, producing for export some of the finest vegetables in the Middle East. Cattle and poultry were installed, dairy produce, eggs and broiler chickens being marketed in Amman and Beirut as well as on the West Bank. The income from the farm went to the support of a training school for orphan boys from the refugee camps, who received both basic education and acquired special skills such as metal work, electrical engineering, carpentry and so on, as well as training in agriculture. By the time of the June War Musa Alami had 2,000 acres under cultivation, with 160 orphan boys undergoing year round board and training. The war was a disaster for Musa Alami, more than half his land being occupied by the Israeli Army, with the result that its wells were destroyed, 100,000 fruit and shade trees died, and the land went back to desert. But in my experience Musa Alami never gave up hope, and against all odds he has continued his pioneer work even under occupation. I am glad to say that on my recommendation the Norwegian Government has in recent years contributed generously to the upkeep of Musa Alami's project.

Naturally, if there was to be any large-scale resettlement of the refugees this would require massive financial and technical help from outside, though as long as the political uncertainty exists a start in resettling them is unlikely to be made. Yet sometimes, when contemplating what has happened to the Palestinian refugees, my thoughts have turned to the example of Fridtjof Nansen, and I have asked myself whether a man with his strength of personality could not have found a solution, cutting through all the bureaucracy, diplomatic red-tape and international misunderstandings which have bedevilled the problem for generations. The disinheriting of the Palestinian Arabs began with the Balfour Declaration in 1917. Never since then, in spite of President Wilson's Fourteen Points, the Declaration of Human Rights and all the resolutions passed by the General Assembly and Security Council, have they had their heritage restored to them.

*   *   *

After Israel, in the June War, had occupied the whole of what used to be Palestine, the Arabs of Palestine not surprisingly feared that the Israelis had no intention of withdrawing. They saw themselves losing not only all their land but their identity as a national group—something which, indeed, many prominent Israelis tried to deny to them.*

These fears found expression in an extension of guerrilla activities, including the hijacking of planes and terrorist actions such as the attack at Lydda airport and the killings at the Munich Olympic Games. Such actions cannot possibly be defended, though the motive for them can be understood. Indiscriminate terror does no service to the Palestine Arabs' cause, which would be better served by economic or strictly military operations against their enemy. Terror breeds counter-terror and we have seen the Israelis reacting in kind. The killing of a Moroccan in Norway by Israeli intelligence agents has shown my own countryman that no people can now regard themselves as immune from the consequences of this vendetta.

I do not myself believe that Israeli counter-terror will succeed in putting an end to Palestinian terrorism even though it may account for some of its leaders.† The well-known Ameri-

* It was Golda Meir who said of the Palestinians, 'They do not exist.'
† Our own experience in Norway during the Second World War was that a really well-trained and determined sabotage group—as for example that which attacked the heavy water plant at Rjukan—cannot be stopped.

can journalist, I. F. Stone, has called on his 'fellow Jews' to 'recognize that the Arab guerrillas are doing to us what our terrorists and saboteurs of the Irgun, Stern and Haganah did to the British,' and asked them to 'admit that their motives are as honourable as were ours'.

The Jews have seen their dream of a return to their 'National Home' fulfilled. It was Israel Zangwill who coined the slogan 'A land without people for a people without land,' and Theodore Herzl gave no indication that he realized the Zionists would have to deal with a resident Arab population. But that great philosopher Martin Buber has reminded us that when Max Nordau, Herzl's close friend and collaborator, first heard about the Arabs of Palestine he expostulated to Herzl, 'I did not know that! Then we should be doing an injustice!' But Max Nordau's scruples were quickly forgotten. The Zionist movement has consistently ignored the rights of the Palestinian Arabs, and I found many prominent Israelis would refuse to admit that there was such a thing as a Palestinian problem. This is a tragedy, not least for Israel and for Jews in other countries. As I. F. Stone wrote in *The New York Review of Books* on 3 August, 1967: 'How we act towards the Arabs will determine what kind of a people we become: Either oppressors and racists in our turn like those from whom we suffered, or a nobler race, able to transcend the tribal xenophobias which afflict mankind.'

It is therefore disturbing to see that extremists in Israel are not content with the territories which their armies now occupy, but cast greedy eyes over the East Bank of the Jordan as well. Meanwhile, the colonization of Egyptian land in Sinai, of Syrian land in the Golan Heights, and of Palestinian (or Jordanian) land on the West Bank, goes actively ahead, in spite of the requirements of the Geneva Conventions regarding the treatment of occupied territories, and the clear statement in Resolution 242 that 'acquisition of territory by war is "inadmissible".'

The 'secure frontiers', which this resolution calls for and by which Israel, quite naturally, sets so much store, cannot be based on injustice. Moreover, after Israeli forces, both ground and air, have proved their ability to strike deep into the heart of all neighbouring Arab countries, it is now the Arabs who have as much cause as the Israelis to be concerned with the need for security. An effort must be made to raise the debate to a higher level, where common sense, understanding and justice prevail. The aim must be to remove, as far as possible, injustice and suffering for all the peoples of the area, Arabs and Jews alike.

As Glubb Pasha writes in *A Soldier with the Arabs*: 'There is no golden way to peace in Palestine, but without any doubt it is an absolute precondition that the refugee problem be solved by obtaining new dwelling-places, which will provide adequate bases for life. A policy of reprisals and counter-reprisals is destructive for all. Israel will have to make some concessions if she wishes to live in amity with her neighbours, on whom she has inflicted so much suffering. The Arabs have often made mistakes, but the fact that a million have lost their homes and their country cannot be gainsaid.'

Justice in the Middle East means, among other things, that the rights of the Palestinian Arabs must be recognized and that they must be given the opportunity for self-determination in those parts of Palestine which they occupied before the 1967 war—which is, after all, only about 23 per cent of the whole of Palestine in mandate days. The principle of repatriation should be accepted. It would be too much to expect the Israelis simply to move out of the areas and hand them over to the PLO (unless, of course, they had been defeated in another war), and so it would probably be necessary for the areas to be taken into temporary UN trusteeship. All those Palestinians who wish to do so should be enabled to return and become Palestinian citizens. This should be followed by elections for a constituent assembly, to be held under UN supervision, which should be able to decide on the political and economic relations the new Palestinian state should have with its neighbours, Jordan and Israel. Once the constituent assembly had met UN trusteeship should end, though UN troops would have to remain on the ground. It would be natural to expect the new state to give a guarantee that it would be demilitarized, or at any rate that it would in no way represent a military threat to either of its neighbours.

If there is to be agreement between Israel and her neighbours demilitarized zones would have to be established in the Golan Heights and in all or part of Sinai as well, including Sharm el-Sheikh. Our own experience in UNTSO is that these zones must involve UN forces on the ground—observers by themselves are not enough. I would not rule out the possibility of both Arab and Israeli contingents serving under an overall UN command. The only alternative to a UN presence would be a joint policing of the frontiers by troops of the two superpowers, but though in the last resort any peace settlement must depend for its success on active support for it by the United States and the Soviet Union I can hardly see them taking on this rôle. UN forces in demilitarized zones must operate under a mandate from the Security Council which gives them a properly secure position, so that any repetition of a sudden withdrawal, such as we saw in 1967, would be avoided. Ideally the Security Council should itself have the exclusive right to decide when the mission to which its forces were committed had been successfully completed, and thereby to decide the date for their withdrawal. This would probably be difficult to obtain as it would involve infringement on the sovereign rights of the countries concerned.

Regarding what is perhaps the most contentious issue in any settlement between Israel and the Arabs—Jerusalem—I find myself in complete agreement with the proposals which have been put forward by Lord Caradon. This would involve returning Arab Jerusalem to the Palestinians.

EPILOGUE

✳ ✳ ✳ ✳

Since this book was written there has been another major war in the Middle East—the October or Yom Kippur War of 1973. On this occasion it was the Arabs who launched the attack, showing an ability for co-ordinated planning and a courage on the battlefield which surprised the Israeli command and a good deal of neutral opinion as well. On this occasion the Security Council found itself paralysed because of disagreement between the superpowers, both of which arranged a massive airlift to their clients. Fortunately diplomatic contact between the United States and the Soviet Union was maintained, and they eventually combined to secure the passage of a resolution (No. 338), which stated:

The Security Council:
1. Calls upon all parties to the present fighting to cease all firing and terminate all military activity immediately, no later than twelve hours after the moment of the adoption of this decision, in the positions they now occupy.
2. Calls upon the parties concerned to start immediately after the ceasefire the implementation of Security Council Resolution 242 (1967) in all of its parts.
3. Decides that immediately and concurrently with the ceasefire, negotiations start between the parties concerned under appropriate auspices aimed at establishing a just and durable peace in the Middle East.

Negotiations 'under appropriate auspices' began at Geneva on 21 December, the UN Secretary-General taking part as well as representatives of the Governments of Egypt, Israel, Syria,

Jordan, the United States and the Soviet Union. As a result, and following intense personal negotiations by the American Secretary of State, Dr Kissinger, an agreement was reached between Egypt and Israel which resulted in a limited withdrawal by Israeli forces in Sinai. But, to a large extent owing to differences over representation of the Palestinians, a reconvening of the Geneva Conference for the broader problems of peace is, at the time of writing, still awaited.

This agreement also provided for the stationing of US civilian personnel in Sinai to man tactical early warning stations which would supply both sides with advance information of troop movements. This American commitment, which in spite of a good deal of misgiving was approved by both Houses of Congress, is seen by both Egypt and Israel as a particularly valuable form of American involvement.

The Sinai agreement was generally well received in Egypt and Israel. In the rest of the Arab world it aroused considerable misgivings, the Palestinians in particular feeling that they had been left out of consideration. But there is another school of thought which believed that President Sadat had placed himself in a strong position to put pressure on the American Government to work towards a solution based on Security Council Resolutions 242 and 338. During his state visit to America in the autumn of 1975 Sadat appears to have spoken effectively on behalf of the Palestinians.

But the Sinai agreement did present two disturbing factors:

1. It did nothing to halt the Middle East arms race, which is to include more and more deadly weapons. If the Pershing ground-to-ground missile is delivered to Israel by the USA it would tip the balance of power heavily in Israel's favour. Nuclear arms might well be expected to follow, and the consequent danger for a nuclear confrontation in the Middle East would increase.

2. There is nothing in the agreement about the maintenance of the status quo in the occupied areas—i.e. forbidding the setting up of new settlements in the occupied areas as long as the agreement lasts. Israel has accordingly continued to build settlements in these areas, and this makes a final peace agreement even more difficult to obtain. (Israel's withdrawal in Sinai

did not involve the abandonment of a single new settlement.)

For these reasons the time factor is now of supreme importance. It is nine years since the end of the 1967 war. Little progress has been achieved in the search for a political solution for the Middle East. The Palestinians, the most important element and the key to the problem, have for the most part been left out of the discussions.

After the first round of Arab–Israel fighting in 1948 Dr Ralph Bunche, acting as the UN mediator, succeeded in arranging armistice agreements between Israel and her four neighbours —Egypt, Syria, Jordan, and Lebanon. I am myself hopeful that we have progressed since 1949, and that peace-keeping in the Middle East is a more effective instrument than it was in the days of Dr Bunche's great pioneering achievements. In 27 years a new generation of leaders has appeared in all Middle Eastern countries, better educated and perhaps more realistic than their predecessors. I would like to think that these leaders understand that another war cannot solve any of their problems, and that neither would a return to the pre-1967 state of 'no war; no peace'. Only a peace based on justice can be beneficial to all.

The superpowers have shown that they realize this and are prepared to work for it. The implementation of any peace agreement is bound also to require the involvement of the UN. There will have to be sufficient UN forces deployed on the ground to control and supervise any demilitarized zones that are instituted.

One interesting innovation that has already appeared in the 1967 disengagement agreements is that they laid down that all important lines, such as ceasefire lines, buffer zone boundaries, etc., should be marked on the ground. This was not done for the demarcation lines arranged by the 1948 armistices and was a main cause of many of the problems which subsequently arose.

APPENDIX I

✻ ✻ ✻ ✻

RESOLUTION 242 (1967)

Adopted by the Security Council at its 1382nd meeting, on 22 November 1967

The Security Council,

Expressing its continuing concern with the grave situation in the Middle East,

Emphasizing the inadmissibility of the acquisition of territory by war and the need to work for a just and lasting peace in which every State in the area can live in security,

Emphasizing further that all Member States in their acceptance of the Charter of the United Nations have undertaken a commitment to act in accordance with Article 2 of the Charter,

1. *Affirms* that the fulfilment of Charter principles requires the establishment of a just and lasting peace in the Middle East which should include the application of both the following principles:

(i) Withdrawal of Israeli armed forces from territories occupied in the recent conflict;

(ii) Termination of all claims or states of belligerency and respect for and acknowledgement of the sovereignty, territorial integrity and political independence of every State in the area and their right to live in peace within secure and recognized boundaries free from threats or acts of force;

2. *Affirms further* the necessity

(a) For guaranteeing freedom of navigation through international waterways in the area;

(b) For achieving a just settlement of the refugee problem;

(c) For guaranteeing the territorial inviolability and political independence of every State in the area, through measures including the establishment of demilitarized zones;

3. *Requests* the Secretary-General to designate a Special Representative to proceed to the Middle East to establish and maintain contacts with the States concerned in order to promote agreement and assist efforts to achieve a peaceful and accepted settlement in accordance with the provisions and principles in this resolution;

4. *Requests* the Secretary-General to report to the Security Council on the progress of the efforts of the Special Representative as soon as possible.

APPENDIX II

✻✻✻✻

EXTRACTS FROM THE ARMISTICE AGREEMENTS

Israel–Jordan (Article VIII)

1. A Special Committee, composed of two representatives of each Party designated by the respective Governments, shall be established for the purpose of formulating agreed plans and arrangements designed to enlarge the scope of this Agreement and to to effect improvements in its application.

2. The Special Committee shall be organized immediately following the coming into effect of this Agreement and shall direct its attention to the formulation of agreed plans and arrangements for such matters as either Party may submit to it, which, in any case, shall include the following, on which agreement in principle already exists: free movement of traffic on vital roads, including the Bethlehem and Latrun–Jerusalem roads; resumption of the normal functioning of the cultural and humanitarian institutions on Mount Scopus and free access thereto; free access to the Holy Places and cultural institutions and use of the cemetery on the Mount of Olives; resumption of operation of the Latrun pumping station; provision of electricity for the Old City; and resumption of operation of the railroad to Jerusalem.

3. The Special Committee shall have exclusive competence over such matters as may be referred to it. Agreed plans and arrangements formulated by it may provide for the exercise of supervisory functions by the Mixed Armistice Commission established in article XI.

Israel–Syria (Article V)

1. It is emphasized that the following arrangements for the Armistice Demarcation Line between the Israeli and Syrian armed forces and for the Demilitarized Zone are not to be interpreted as having any relation whatsoever to ultimate territorial arrangements affecting the two Parties to this Agreement.

2. In pursuance of the spirit of the Security Council resolution of 16 November 1948, the Armistice Demarcation Line and the Demilitarized Zone have been defined with a view toward separating the armed forces to the two Parties in such manner as to minimize the possibility of friction and incident, while providing for the gradual restoration of normal civilian life in the area of the Demilitarized Zone, without prejudice to the ultimate settlement.

3. The Armistice Demarcation Line shall be as delineated on the map attached to this Agreement as annex I. The Armistice Demarcation Line shall follow a line midway between the existing truce lines, as certified by the United Nations Truce Supervision Organization for the Israeli and Syrian forces. Where the existing truce lines run along the international Boundary between Syria and Palestine, the Armistice Demarcation Line shall follow the boundary line.

4. The armed forces of the two Parties shall nowhere advance beyond the Armistice Demarcation Line.

5. (a) Where the Armistice Demarcation Line does not correspond to the international boundary between Syria and Palestine, the area between the Armistice Demarcation Line and the boundary, pending final territorial settlement between the Parties, shall be established as a Demilitarized Zone from which the armed forces of both Parties shall be totally excluded, and in which no activities by military or para-military forces shall be permitted. This provision applies to the Ein Gev and Dardara sectors which shall form part of the Demilitarized Zone.

(b) Any advance by the armed forces, military or para-military, of either Party into any part of the Demilitarized Zone, when confirmed by the United Nations representatives referred to in the following subparagraph, shall constitute a flagrant violation of this Agreement.

(c) The Chairman of the Mixed Armistice Commission established in article VII of this Agreement and United Nations observers attached to the Commission shall be responsible for ensuring the full implementation of this article.

(d) The withdrawal of such armed forces as are now found in the Demilitarized Zone shall be in accordance with the schedule of withdrawal annexed to this Agreement (annex II).

(e) The Chairman of the Mixed Armistice Commission shall be empowered to authorize the return of civilians to villages and settlements in the Demilitarized Zone and the employment of limited numbers of *locally* recruited civilian police in the zone for internal security purposes, and shall be guided in this regard by the schedule of withdrawal referred to in subparagraph (d) of this article.

6. On each side of the Demilitarized Zone there shall be areas, as defined in annex III to this Agreement, in which defensive forces only shall be maintained, in accordance with the definition of defensive forces set forth in annex IV to this Agreement.

Egypt–Israel (Article VIII)

1. The area comprising the village of El Auja and vicinity, as defined in paragraph 2 of this Article, shall be demilitarized, and both Egyptian and Israeli armed forces shall be totally excluded therefrom. The Chairman of the Mixed Armistice Commission established in Article X of this Agreement and United Nations Observers attached to the Commission shall be responsible for ensuring the full implementation of this provision.

2. The area thus demilitarized shall be as follows: From a point on the Egypt–Palestine frontier five (5) kilometres north-west of the intersection of the Rafah-El Auja road and the frontier (MR 08750468), south-east to Khashm El Mamdud (MR 09650414), thence south-east to Hill 405 (MR 10780285), thence south-west to a point on the Egypt–Palestine frontier

five (5) kilometres south-east of the intersection of the old railway tracks and the frontier (MR 09950145), thence returning north-west along the Egypt–Palestine frontier to the point of origin.

3. On the Egyptian side of the frontier, facing the El Auja area, no Egyptian defensive positions shall be closer to El Auja than El Qouseima and Abou Aoueigila.

4. The road Taba-Qouseima-Auja shall not be employed by any military forces whatsoever for the purpose of entering Palestine.

5. The movement of armed forces of either Party to this Agreement into any part of the area defined in paragraph 2 of this Article, for any purpose, or failure by either Party to respect or fulfil any of the other provisions of this Article, when confirmed by the United Nations representatives, shall constitute a flagrant violation of this Agreement.

MOUNT SCOPUS AGREEMENT

It is hereby jointly agreed that

1. The area as delineated on the attached map will be assigned to United Nations protection until hostilities cease or a new agreement is entered upon. It shall include the areas designated as Hadassah Hospital, Hebrew University, Augusta Victoria and the Arab village of Issawiya. The United Nations agree to become a signatory to this document by representation through the Senior Observer in the Jerusalem area and the Chairman of the Truce Commission. It therefore accepts responsibility for the security of this area as described herewith.

2. There shall be a no-man's-land location extending for approximately 200 yards along the main road between the Augusta Victoria and the Hebrew University Buildings, with suitable checkposts established at each end. Other checkposts will be established on the Perimeter of the zone under protection, and all parties agree that access desired should be along the main road via the United Nations checkposts as established by the United Nations Commander. All other attempts at entry

will be considered as unlawful invasion and treated accordingly.

3. In their respective areas armed Arab and Jewish civilian police will be placed on duty under the United Nations Commander. The United Nations flag will fly on the main buildings. All military personnel of both sides will be withdrawn this day, together with their equipment and such supplies as are not required by the United Nations Commander.

4. The United Nations will arrange that both parties receive adequate supplies of food and water. Replacements of necessary personnel in residence on Mount Scopus will be scheduled by the United Nations Commander. Visits of properly accredited individuals will also be arranged by the United Nations Commander in consultation with each party in respect of its area. The United Nations undertakes to limit the population on Mount Scopus to those individuals needed for its operation, plus the present population of the village of Issawiya. No addition will be made to the village population except by agreement of both parties. The initial personnel roster of civilian police in the Jewish section shall not exceed a total of 85. The civilian personnel attached thereto shall not exceed a total of 33. The Arab civilian population at Augusta Victoria shall not exceed a total of 40.

5. It is hereby agreed by both parties that the area is not to be used as a base for military operations, nor will it be attacked or unlawfully entered upon.

6. In the event that the Arab Legion withdraws from the area, the United Nations Commander is to be given sufficient advanced notice in writing in order that satisfactory arrangements may be made to substitute for this protocol another agreement.

(Signed)
LASH (Arab Military Commander)
SHALTIEL (Jewish Military Commander)
NIEUWENHUYS (Chairman, UN Truce Commission)
BRUNSSON (Senior Observer, Mediator's Jerusalem Group)
(S/3015, 25 May 1953)

APPENDIX III

✻ ✻ ✻ ✻

Lt. General Odd Bull   23 July 1970
Chief of Staff
United Nations Truce Supervision
    Organization in Palestine
Jerusalem

Dear General Bull,

Now that, for personal reasons, you find it necessary to leave your post as Chief of Staff of the United Nations Truce Supervision Organization in Palestine, I want to express to you my deep appreciation of the service you have rendered to the United Nations over the past seven years. Much as I regret your decision not to continue with UNTSO, I can assure you that I fully appreciate the reasons for it and I can well imagine that after seven years in the Middle East you may wish for a change of pace and environment.

You have occupied for those years one of the most delicate and demanding posts in the United Nations Secretariat through a period when the conditions have been anything but promising. During the time of your United Nations service in Jerusalem there have been a series of crises in the Middle East, of which the climactic one was, of course, the Arab–Israel war of June 1967. UNTSO has been intimately involved in these crises, and the very nature of the whole operation has been changed by them. Especially in the past two years, the military observers under your direction have served in increasingly dangerous and difficult conditions, and I know that this anxiety has been a heavy additional burden for you to carry, as it has also been for us here.

The United Nations has been fortunate indeed to have had you in Jerusalem during these critical years. The fact that this has been for all of us an increasingly frustrating period in which the United Nations has often found itself unable to do what the situation seemed to require, does not detract from the importance of the United Nations presence in the Middle East which UNTSO represents, nor does it detract from the necessity of maintaining and conducting the United Nations operation in the hope that things may improve in the future. To conduct the affairs of UNTSO amid the conflicting emotions, tensions and controversies of the situation in the Middle East, requires the sound judgement and the steady hand which have characterized your service. I may add that I regard as by no means the least of your achievements the fact that you have managed to the last to maintain excellent relations with all of the Governments and authorities concerned, so that UNTSO continues to be respected and trusted by them.

I extend to you and to Mrs. Bull my warmest good wishes for your future happiness.

Yours sincerely,

U Thant
Secretary-General

INDEX

✻ ✻ ✻ ✻

RAF (Royal Air Force), 27
Red Sea, 125, 136
Reichert, Capt, 74, 75
Riad, Gen Abdel Munim, 159
Riad, Gen Mahmoud, 108, 114*,
    134, 149, 161
Rifai, Samir, 25
Rikhye, Maj-Gen I. J., 89, 106,
    107, 113, 116
Riley, Gen, 64, 65, 173
Rittby, Capt, 18
Rogers, William, 172
Rosenius, Lt-Col Carl O., 134, 136,
    139, 170
Royal Netherlands Air Force,
    112*
Ryan, Pat, 116

Saatvedt, Ivor, 26
Sadat, President, 189
Said, Nuri es-, 7, 11
Salam, Saab, 6, 13, 15
Sasson, Moshe, 91, 100, 102
Shibbly, 10, 11
Shukeiry, Ahmed, 72, 73, 93, 101
Siilasvuo, Col E., 144, 170, 171,
    174
Sion, Col Dov, 137, 145
Skattum, O. J., 29
Skinner, Major Roy, 134, 139, 170
Smith, Ditlev, 30, 31
Solh, Sami es-, 6, 7, 14
Sollenberg, Capt, 18
Sparre, Capt E. S., 96, 102
Spiller, Capt, 33
Spinelli, Pier, 89
Stanaway, Lt-Col M., 89, 100, 105,
    118, 141
Steen, Capt Erik Anker, 33
Stone, I. F., 185
Suez Canal, 41, 123, 125, 130,
    132–44, 156, 178
Suez Canal Authority, 136, 140,
    148, 150, 151
Suez War, 1956, 20, 24, 40, 56,
    127
Sweidani, Gen, 95, 123, 138, 156

Tabor, Hans, 110, 119
TA line, 168
Tel, Wasfi, 80, 82, 85
Thant, U, 38, 39, 83, 96, 107–11,

119, 138, 140, 142, 155, 158,
    162, 165, 166, 169, 172
Tiberias, Lake, disputed fishing
    rights, 44, 45, 52
Tlass, Gen M., 156
Toukan, M. A., 105
Trappist Monastery, 60
Tun, Lt-Col Sein, 170

UAR (United Arab Republic), 24,
    25, 106, 107
UN Commission of Enquiry on
    Palestine, 1947, 142
UNDP (United Nations Develop-
    ment Programme), 146, 158
UNEF (United Nations Emergency
    Force), xv, 40, 56, 92, 95, 101,
    104, 106–8, 111, 112, 121,
    124, 137, 177, 178
UNFICYP (United Nations Force
    in Cyprus), 144, 178
UN General Assembly, 47, 107,
    122, 130, 178, 180, 184
UN General Assembly Res. A
    181(11) of 29 Nov. 1947, 42
    (internationalization of Jeru-
    salem)
    Res. 1237 (ES-iii), 16 (withdrawal
    of US forces from Lebanon)
UNOGIL (United Nations Obser-
    ver Group in Lebanon), 1–27
UN peacekeeping efforts, 19, 27
UN peacekeeping, lessons learnt,
    176
UN Secretary-General, 24, 25, 41,
    46, 54, 65, 68, 79, 80, 84, 89,
    100–2, 106–11, 113, 116, 118,
    120, 121, 124, 130, 132, 135,
    139, 142, 147–50, 152–5, 161,
    163, 166, 170, 171, 175, 181,
    188, 192
UN Security Council, 1, 19, 55, 56,
    60, 68, 76, 84, 101, 107, 109,
    110, 117–24, 130, 132, 133,
    152–4, 156, 158, 163–5, 178,
    184, 187
UN Security Council Res S/902 of
    15 July 1948, 7, 40, (Super-
    vision of ceasefire by UNTSO)
    Res 235 of 9 June 1967, 152
    (ceasefire in Jordan valley)
    Res 242 of 22 Nov 1967, 123,